T0128034

# It's All Your Fault

## Your Life, Your Choice

### DEIDRE WILTON

**BALBOA.**
PRESS

A DIVISION OF HAY HOUSE

Balboa Press books may be ordered through booksellers or by contacting:

Balboa Press
A Division of Hay House
1663 Liberty Drive
Bloomington, IN 47403
www.balboapress.com.au
1 (877) 407-4847

Because of the dynamic nature of the Internet, any web addresses or
links contained in this book may have changed since publication and
may no longer be valid. The views expressed in this work are solely those
of the author and do not necessarily reflect the views of the publisher,
and the publisher hereby disclaims any responsibility for them.

The author of this book does not dispense medical advice or prescribe the use
of any technique as a form of treatment for physical, emotional, or medical
problems without the advice of a physician, either directly or indirectly. The
intent of the author is only to offer information of a general nature to help
you in your quest for emotional and spiritual well-being. In the event you use
any of the information in this book for yourself, which is your constitutional
right, the author and the publisher assume no responsibility for your actions.

Any people depicted in stock imagery provided by Getty Images are
models, and such images are being used for illustrative purposes only.
Certain stock imagery © Getty Images.

Print information available on the last page.

ISBN: 978-1-5043-1378-0 (sc)
ISBN: 978-1-5043-1381-0 (e)

Balboa Press rev. date: 10/02/2018

# DEDICATIONS

This book is dedicated to everyone who is awakening.

May your soul's journey be magical, and may you always find the courage and determination to face what you fear.

# CONTENTS

Dedications . . . . . . . . . . . . . . . . . . . . . . . . . . . . . . . . . v

Introduction . . . . . . . . . . . . . . . . . . . . . . . . . . . . . .ix

Chapter 1   My Journey To Awareness . . . . . . . . . . . . . . . 1

Chapter 2   Ego Self vs Higher Self . . . . . . . . . . . . . . . . 7

Chapter 3   The Importance of Self-Love. . . . . . . . . . . . . . 10

Chapter 4   The Spider's Web . . . . . . . . . . . . . . . . . . . . 12

Chapter 5   Choosing Your Life . . . . . . . . . . . . . . . . . . . 18

Chapter 6   The Earth Plane – Our School of Learning . . . . . 27

Chapter 7   Your Natal Chart – Your Blue Print. . . . . . . . . . 35

Chapter 8   The Sun Signs . . . . . . . . . . . . . . . . . . . . . . 38

Chapter 9   The Ascendant or Rising Sign . . . . . . . . . . . . . 52

Chapter 10  The Moon Signs. . . . . . . . . . . . . . . . . . . . . 58

Chapter 11  Saturn – Becoming a Grown-Up . . . . . . . . . . . 68

Chapter 12  Uranus Opposition – Mid-Life Crisis Time . . . . . 81

Chapter 13  Chiron – The Wounded Healer. . . . . . . . . . . . . 90

Chapter 14  The Many Layers Of Learning . . . . . . . . . . . . 100

Chapter 15  Your Spiritual Helpers and Past Lives . . . . . . . . 104

Chapter 16  The Star Child. . . . . . . . . . . . . . . . . . . . . . 110

Chapter 17  The Mirrors Around You. . . . . . . . . . . . . . . . 112

Chapter 18  The Power Of Detachment . . . . . . . . . . . . . . . 114

Chapter 19  Finding The Real You . . . . . . . . . . . . . . . . . 117

Acknowledgements . . . . . . . . . . . . . . . . . . . . . . . . . . 119

About The Author . . . . . . . . . . . . . . . . . . . . . . . . . . 121

# INTRODUCTION

*("What was I thinking?!")*

The title of this book "It's All Your Fault" is a two-fold awareness. Firstly, it's all your fault because YOU chose your life before you were born – you chose your parents, your neighbours, your school mates, your best friends, your partners, your jobs, the countries and towns you live in, your talents, your strengths, and of course your challenges and weaknesses too. And you chose all of this to LEARN from. Unfortunately, in the process of your "arriving" on the earth plane, you lost the Hand Book of what you chose and so you entered this lifetime with no conscious knowledge of any of these choices. But they are there, inside your soul and your Higher Self and, even better, written into your astrological Natal or Birth Chart *(see page 34)*.

The second reason it's all your fault is that once you are here on the earth plane, you have the ability to choose how you react to all that life throws at you. In every moment of every day that you live here, you have the choice to see and experience what is happening in your life from a perspective of fear and emotional overload, or from the perspective of learning and understanding. For so long as you choose to see all that happens to you as an external force that you have no control over, you are a powerless victim stuck on the emotional roller coaster of life. All you experience makes you feel like you have no control over your life, and therefore the Ego will **instruct** you to blame everything and everyone around you, which in turn strips you of your personal power and leaves you like a pawn on the chess board of life – feeling used, abused and completely stuck in victim mentality. Not only does living your life in this way bring you no true happiness or peace, this emotional turmoil is also the cause of most of the illnesses, accidents, and dis-eases you suffer from. The late great Louise Hay pioneered for us the understanding that every emotion we feel is directly linked to a part of our body. Everything we feel and experience in this life is absorbed by us, and what goes in must come out. And the easiest way for the body to release anything is physically. If you hold onto resentment and anger, your body will need to release it, and will do so through your skin and your liver. If you spend your life carrying the burdens of everyone else or feeling that your life is one big burden, without a doubt your shoulders will suffer from this. And if you refuse to go with the flow of life and allow your soul to guide you, your hips and "mobility" will suffer. (Hence why so many souls, who do not wish to change or "modernise" themselves as they age, end up having hip replacements in today's society.)

None of this needs to happen if you can just change your perspective to truly and deeply understand that you are here to LEARN. You are NOT here to suffer – but the humanness of us can use suffering to learn. It doesn't have to be this way. We can learn so much through love and joy too, if we allow ourselves to do so. But the very nature of the earth plane is to teach us the hard way until we can accept and learn in a more gentle, evolved and spiritual manner.

The purpose of this book is to introduce you to the world of metaphysics and astrology, where all the answers for who you truly are and what your purpose on the earth plane is can be answered. You are here by choice and not by chance, and there is plenty of help, support and guidance available to you. You chose this life and every facet of it long before you were born, and your mission is to take responsibility for this, every step of the way. When you do so, you choose to co-create with the Universe and you can then honour and love yourself for the beautiful, talented and powerful soul that you are. You are a soul on a journey - a spirit having a human experience - and all that you go through, learn and be in any given lifetime has been pre-destined and chosen by you. We are all here for this same purpose, yet we all have our own paths to walk and our own lessons to learn.

So, are you ready to stop banging your head against a brick wall and get off that crazy emotional roller coaster ride we call "life"? Are you ready to start living and loving the life you have chosen? If yes, then this book is for you. Please read on and open yourself up to all that you can BE.

# CHAPTER 1

# MY JOURNEY TO AWARENESS

*("Or more fondly known as – bringing me to my knees.")*

I was 23 years old the first time someone said to me, "Everything that happens in your life is all your fault".

At the time I was mortified at the thought! How could all those dreadful things other people had done to me, all those heart-breaking experiences, and all those random events possibly be my fault? Twenty-three year-old me thought, "This woman has absolutely no idea of who I am and what I have been through. She has no idea what she is talking about!"

Little did I know it at the time that this was the first true introduction to my Ego Self. In fact, it was another 18 years before I could even begin to accept this statement and to understand the journey of the soul on the earth plane.

During those 18 years, I travelled the world, had various jobs and careers, fell in love with a man or two, fell out of love with a man or two, had two beautiful daughters – all the normal stuff. I also became more and more stressed and more and more unhappy. I had no idea why or what was wrong with me. The mental and emotional stress I was feeling created physical reactions in my body such as migraine headaches and digestion problems. The inability to find peace within myself started to manifest itself as pain and sickness throughout my physical body. What I did not know then is that all that we feel, experience and go through in life is absorbed into us and therefore must also be released as well. What goes in must come out. And the easiest way for the human body to release anything negative within it is through pain and dis-ease.

All my life I had a fascination with metaphysics, astrology, clairvoyance and crystals and all my life I knew things about people, situations and what would happen next.

As a child and young person, I blurted these things out readily and haphazardly, and found myself in hot water for this time and time again; it seemed others did not like it when you knew too much about them, or when you revealed things about them that they did not want to know themselves. And so, I shut it down. I stopped listening to those thoughts and awarenesses and this is when the stress and the unhappiness with myself began to grow. I knew deep inside that I had a purpose in this lifetime and I also knew that I was very very protected – yet still I did not "get" or pursue that missing link. I had many extraordinary life experiences. When I look back at them now, I am amazed that I didn't wake up sooner. But to me in that past time and space, such things were normal and so I just kept plodding along in my increasingly uncomfortable "comfort zone", lost and unwell and with very little internal peace.

When I was around the age of 38 (the beginning of my Uranus opposition or mid-life crisis), those in the higher planes (upstairs) decided that, as it was part of my Contract with Spirit for this lifetime, enough was enough; they brought me to my knees to force me to change direction. It was hard – extremely hard. I had moved with my partner and two pre-school daughters to a smallish town in New Zealand and I was the breadwinner for our family. My employers at the time decided that they did not like me or want me to work for them anymore. Rather than fire me or ask me to leave, they labelled me a thief and did so publicly, in a way that they hoped would ensure that I would never work in that town again. I was not a thief – and I was horrified, angry, upset and broken by what they did and what they said about me. This was one of the greatest life lessons of my life, as it completely ripped apart my self-confidence, my abilities and talents within that career, and how I valued myself as a person. Fortunately for me at that time, I had gotten to know others in that small town who did trust in me and who would employ me. These other people believed in me and gave me work and it came to light that my ex-employers had somewhat of a reputation for treating their employees badly.

It was at this time that I met the woman who would change my life by becoming my friend, spiritual teacher and mentor for 14 years, before her passing on my birthday in 2016. Margaret McElroy (or Margaret Birken as she was known back then) was an amazing woman and a deep trance channel for the Ascended Master Maitreya (www.maitreya.co). Anyone who had the good fortune to have a Reading, become a student, or be present at one of her channelling events will know the incredible energy that this woman possessed and what this energy could do to bring change and awareness into your life. Margaret was indeed a Master on this earth plane and I am proud to be carrying on the work that she started, along with many other of her graduate students from around the world.

Margaret taught me about the Ascended Masters and how closely they work with us on the earth plane. This group of highly evolved Beings introduced themselves to humanity over one hundred years ago, and they have dedicated their existence to helping and guiding us ever since. Through their knowledge and unconditional love, they help us to learn, evolve and ascend through our many lifetimes here. These Beings are called "Masters" because they have mastered life on the earth plane in the few incarnations they had here. They understand what it feels like and how it is to live on the earth plane, as well as knowing and understanding the energy of the spiritual planes where they reside; and so they are the best equipped out of all the Ascended Beings in the Spiritual Realms to assist us and guide us along our soul journeys. There are many Masters in the Spirit world, but only a small group can call themselves Ascended Masters. These Beings were once upon a time known on the earth plane as the likes of Mary Magdalene, Buddha, Jesus and Mother Mary. Once they learned all that they needed to from their time here, they ascended to the highest spiritual planes to watch over and assist us whenever possible. But as with all spiritual energies, they can only watch and guide us where possible as they may not EVER interfere with our "free will".

The Master Maitreya is known as the "world teacher" and so those who work with him, and are familiar with his energy, are also here to teach, guide and assist humanity towards creating heaven on earth. The energy of unconditional love and support that these Beings bring to us is incredible, and anyone who has ever had the privilege of sitting in their energy will know how wonderful this feels and how life-changing it can be.

Margaret and I were friends before she became my teacher and so we established a wonderful relationship which lasted here on the earth plane until her passing. By the time Margaret came into my life, I had become aware that my "thinking" was NOT the same as everyone else's. I had undergone some training, and I had started giving Clairvoyant Readings using Tarot Cards. One day Margaret offered to do an Astrological Reading for me which was something I had never experienced before. I, like many of you, never went past reading about my "Star Sign" when any such information was presented and, of course, read my Daily Horoscope in the Newspaper etc. That was really the limit of my knowledge... or so I thought.

Within minutes of Margaret laying eyes on my Chart she exclaimed, "Oh my goodness you are an Astrologer! You have been one lifetime after lifetime and you are here to do this once again."

I was gobsmacked, to say the least! I sat there looking at my Natal Chart with all its symbols, circles, colours and glyphs and thought to myself, "She must be joking. This makes no sense to me whatsoever."

However, as Margaret continued to talk and the energy of the Master Maitreya enveloped me, I felt and heard an audible "click" inside my head. The soul memory was activated; the right key had been found to unlock the gifts and talents that lay hidden within me. To my delight and total amazement, within just a few short weeks I was able to understand Astrology. I am blessed with many many incarnations of astrological knowledge on an intuitive and esoteric level. Since that day I have lived by it and use it to help myself and thousands of others to understand who they truly are, and how to navigate their life paths through understanding their own personal astrology.

About one year after this, my mother was shifting house and therefore cleaning out all the bits and pieces belonging to myself and my brothers that she had kept over the years. One of the things she found was the first ever "school project" I did at the age of around nine. That entire project was about Astrology!

I have been highly intuitive and highly sensitive since the day I was born. However, I had no conscious realisation of this until I was 38 years of age. For many many years, I thought that everybody knew things about everyone else. I would say things out loud that I knew and felt with various reactions: being told I had an "overactive imagination"; horror and anger from those who felt I was exposing them in some way; tears of relief that someone actually "got" what that they were feeling or going through. I remember having readings with various Clairvoyants and Mediums in New Zealand and around the world during my late teens and twenties, thinking how cool it would be to be like them and able to see and know such things. I could not see that I not only had the ability to do the same thing, I was already doing it!

This brought me to my theory that what we do as children, particularly in our play time or in our own time, is what we are here to do as adults. Children naturally gravitate towards what they are good at and what they enjoy, and the things they do in this space are, more often than not, their true life path and destiny. From a very young age children are already demonstrating and showing the world the direction they are here to move in. Unfortunately, often once the "conditioning" of society and parents kicks in, the soul moves away from such things. It is not until they reach their late thirties that they remember what they used to love to do, and can then work towards embracing that knowledge and awareness once again.

## CHAPTER 2

# EGO SELF VS HIGHER SELF

*("Let the battles begin.")*

We come to the earth plane as purely spiritual beings to grow and learn through the human experiences offered to us here. The earth plane is a School of Learning. Yet most of us experience it as a crazy roller coaster ride of emotions until we learn to master the Ego Self.

We are each made up of a Lower Self/Ego and connection to the earth plane, and a Higher Self/Spirit and connection to the spiritual realms. Ego is your base energy and your original fight or flight mode. This is a necessary part of human make-up that enables you to know when you are in danger and how to act because of this. It is the human survival instinct and has an important purpose in your life. However, it cannot and must not be allowed to be in charge of all that you believe, all that you feel and all that you see. Your Ego Self wants power and it learned a long time ago that the best way to have power is to create drama, unhappiness, and fear, because these are things that it is experienced in and knows best. For so long as the Ego Self is calling the shots in your life it will keep you in your comfort zone, it will stop you from growing emotionally and spiritually, and worst of all it will keep you in complete fear of the future and of all that has gone before in your life. It can be likened to a guard dog, whereby it believes it has one task and that is to keep you safe, and to do so it will create as much noise, disruption and fear as possible within you and around you, so as you will not move forward, change or evolve in life. Your Ego is an extremely powerful tool, but it cannot be allowed to be the boss of all that you think and feel; your Ego must be kept on a very short leash.

The Higher Self is your connection to the Spirit world. This part of you has total and utter faith that you will always be looked after, and you will always be loved. It does not need to know what's going to happen tomorrow, because it knows that whatever does happen tomorrow is meant to be and is part of your journey. It also does not worry about yesterday, because it is fully aware that what has gone before cannot be changed or altered in any way, so why go back there? Only in the present moment do we have all the resources and power to act or react.

This does not mean that we are supposed to go through life without any thought, planning, or hindsight. All of these things are necessary tools for us to use during our human experience, but we are here to use them to educate ourselves, to raise our awareness and to co-create with the Universe. You see, the Universe has the big picture; it knows exactly what you are going to do, when, and why. However we only get to know things on a "need to know basis"; for if we were to know from day one all the things we chose to go through and be, we would probably run a mile in the other direction, refuse to attempt any of it, and therefore learn nothing from our experience on the earth plane.

The challenge is to control the Ego Self by learning to slowly but surely detach from it and its power over you. The first step in learning to do this is to become aware of every thought that goes through your head. Start really paying attention to your mind and where your thought patterns take you, what you are mainly thinking about, and what your default thought settings are. We often have places in our mind that, like a dog with a bone, we just keep going back to for one more chew. Nine times out of ten, that place is not a happy one, especially when your Ego is controlling your thoughts. We all use the same basic process within our minds whereby the thought evokes the emotion which then creates the action.

*"The thought evokes the emotion which then creates the action."*

What we have to do is get to the root of the cause which is the initial "thought". As you become more and more aware of what is going on in your head, you will start to see patterns of behaviour that relate to certain thoughts, and you will see physical responses in your body as other thoughts take power in your head. Watch and observe all of this within you as you go about your day. You don't need to do anything but this, and as you do so you teach yourself to be the observer of yourself and all that you are thinking, feeling and doing. The more you observe the more you can detach and see yourself through the eyes of your Higher Self.

As you continue to observe and become more aware of the feelings and emotions inside of you and what they encourage you to do and be, you can start to gently question these things to see if they are for your highest good, or if they are the result of fears that you no longer need to hold on to. One by one, little by little, you can start to override the negative thinking and the fear thoughts, by realising that they have no real basis. You have the power to overcome anything that originates in your own mind. YOU are in charge of what you think. It is solely and completely your responsibility to filter and limit your thoughts so as the resulting feelings they create are positive and constructive ones. From here the actions you take will always be for your highest good, and for the highest good of all others concerned.

Living and loving your life on the earth plane is about taking back the power that you give away every moment of every day by allowing thoughts that have no positive purpose in your life to have control over you. Do not ever doubt that you are not only the master of your destiny but the master of all that you think along the way as well.

# CHAPTER 3

# THE IMPORTANCE OF SELF-LOVE

*("Learning to love yourself – wobbly bits and all.")*

Your Ego self is a bully and a tyrant when you allow it to be in control of you. It revels in your insecurities, your weaknesses, your fears and your past mistakes. It allows you to think and believe that what you did yesterday will be what you do tomorrow, not wanting you to change, ascend, evolve or grow. It likes you right under its thumb no matter how unpleasant or uncomfortable this is for you. However, it is also a necessary part of you.

The greatest challenge we face on the earth plane, as souls here to learn, is often not the trials and tribulations we chose to experience but our inner fears and insecurities. The power that these feelings and beliefs have over us is incredible, and can keep us stuck in one place, in one state of mind and in one perspective, for any given amount of time. The things we say to ourselves inside of our own heads, or even out loud sometimes, are things we would not dream of saying to or even thinking of another soul. Yet we readily, consciously and deliberately speak to ourselves in such a way on a daily basis. If you stop to think about this, you can really see the injustice of it. What gives you the right to be so judgemental, critical and downright mean to yourself? It is unnecessary, detrimental to your health and wellbeing, as well as a complete and utter waste of your energy and intelligence. And it really is just not fair. Every thought creates energy. When you are constantly bombarding yourself with destructive thought patterns and bullying yourself in a way that you would never consider bullying another human being, you are channelling completely negative energy at yourself that can cause damage in many different ways. You must learn to understand that you did nothing wrong when you made a choice that didn't work out positively, or when a decision you made turns out to be not as in your favour as you thought it would be. You are here to learn – nothing more, nothing less. And the best way to learn is often to get it wrong and fail. How can you truly measure your success if you have not had failure to put it up against? And how can you know real happiness and peace until you have felt deep sorrow and anger? Sometimes, life is as much about eliminating choices as it is about making them.

Everything in our lives comes back to the one basic principle of self-love. Without the power of this energy, life is a struggle, full of self-doubt and judgement.

# CHAPTER 4

# THE SPIDER'S WEB

## *("Be the web and not the fly.")*

As a new soul on the earth plane, you are full of purity. You are not born with any awareness of discrimination, bias or judgement. You are an open vessel that from an early age starts to fill up with all that is presented to you. In fact, by around the age of three, a child has already established whether or not they feel safe, whether or not they are secure, and who they can rely on to take care of them and answer their needs.

We choose our lives before we are born; there are no accidents and no mistakes. We choose what we need to learn as a soul evolving through its journey to enlightenment and everything we choose to learn is brought to us through the experiences we choose, the people we choose to teach us, and the many paths that we choose to walk to reach our destiny. The one thing we have on the earth plane that is solely of our own making is "free will". This is the one thing that Spirit cannot interfere with in our lives. So, when I say that we choose our lives before we are born, I mean that we choose to go from A to Z. However, to get from A – Z there are many different paths to choose from once we are here, and it is these many and varied paths that are our free will. No matter who is on them or what we experience along the way, all of these paths lead to the same destination and will allow us to experience the same learning, albeit in different ways.

If I was to paint a picture of this for you, it would look like a giant spider's web whereby everything that happens in your life, sparks a reaction that affects the next connecting piece of silk thread. As we make decisions and choices in our lives every day, there are consequences and they send out energetic vibrations through the giant spider's web to touch on and affect us and the lives of other people as well. This is because we are all part of the oneness, or the one spider's web – interacting, touching, affecting and influencing the lives of others as we grow and learn.

The first and most important things that we choose for a life on the earth plane are our parents and family. We choose our parents for two extremely important reasons. Firstly, we need their DNA and their ancestral make-up to give us a basis to develop ourselves from. With the DNA and genetic make-up of our parents, we can, for instance, integrate the lessons for health issues that can be presented as hereditary weaknesses. For example, if we choose to be raised in a lower socio-economic family and environment, then there will be restrictions, limitations, and conditioning that we are choosing to learn from, things that we could not learn from a wealthy family. As the late great Louise Hay taught the world – every illness, physical weakness, and dis-ease is associated with an emotional or mental condition or influence, which can be brought about by our upbringing, the conditioning we receive growing up and of course our genetic inheritances.

Secondly, we choose our parents because, in most cases, they have us under their major influence and control until we are around the age of six years old. In this day and age, many children spend a lot of time in Day Care Facilities, as parents need to work to provide the material things necessary to survive. But even if they spend a lot of time in such places, it is still the parents, or the major caregiver, that the children come home to during those early years and who mould them and develop them the most through the early stages of life on the earth plane. This moulding is what is known as "conditioning".

We cannot help but condition our children as parents. We put our values, our beliefs and our fears on to them deliberately and non-deliberately. It is this early conditioning that we know we will receive when we choose the souls who will be our parents; we choose this for reasons that are all to do with the development of our soul and its journey to enlightenment and ascension. In many cases, how we are treated and conditioned as children can become a lifelong mission for us to change. This too is relevant to our soul's journey and it is all necessary for our soul growth. Remember a lot of what we choose to experience in life is for us to know what NOT to do, as well as to know what TO do.

Once the soul chooses its parents and enters the womb of the soul it has chosen to be its mother in this lifetime, it has three months to decide; right time, right place, right parents. If it finds during this three month period that it is not going to learn what it needs to learn for its own soul growth at this time, it has the choice to take itself back to Spirit where it can wait with the same parents for a better time, or where it may choose a new set of parents – or a different father or mother. This return to Spirit is what we call miscarriages and terminations on the earth plane. Please always know that the choice to have a termination or abortion is made by the new soul entering the body, in conjunction with the souls of the parents; it is NOT made by the conscious mind of the mother or father, even though this is how it may feel or seem to be. We reincarnate on the earth plane to LEARN and if we cannot learn what we know we need to, then we wait – just like a seed waiting for the soil and conditions to be perfect to germinate. Once the soul has been born on the earth plane, it again has three months to decide; right time, right place, right parents. And if it feels that it cannot learn or evolve with the choices it made at that time, it is free once again to return to Spirit to wait for the ideal conditions to present themselves. This is known as our "cot deaths" or SIDS (Sudden Infant Death Syndrome). This transition back to the spirit world can also be caused by illness or accidents at the young one to three month age period, and this is where I would like you to once again imagine that giant spider's web that we are all a part of.

To become fully evolved and enlightened a soul chooses to go through every experience it can possibly think of that will bring forth the emotions, the reactions, the changes and the results necessary for its growth. We are all part of the oneness or Universal God Energy, so what affects me in my life will affect you in yours – one way or another. And the closer to one another we are in the giant spider's web, the more strongly we will feel the choices and reactions of those around us.

So, let's go back to the new-born baby who arrives on the earth plane to start the next stage of its soul journey. Perhaps this soul arrives here and realises at around two months old that she has made the wrong choice as she cannot learn what she needs to (what she planned before she was born) if she stays the daughter of these particular parents, at this particular time, and in this particular place. So she chooses to take herself back to Spirit. Perhaps rather than a cot death, she decides on that deep soul level and in conjunction with the Lords of Karma and all the other soul consciousnesses of those close to her in the spider's web, to pass over as the result of a car accident. In choosing this way, the spider's web is being activated so the learning from this experience becomes a lesson for ALL involved. Perhaps, the driver of the car that caused the accident was drunk and had chosen in his Contract for life on the earth plane to have a drinking problem that unless addressed would result in him taking a life and facing the consequences. He may have brought the addiction with him from another lifetime or developed it purposefully (in accordance with his Contract) in this lifetime. He would have been given numerous opportunities to overcome this through help from those around him whom he chose to have in his life, but he did not listen to or accept their help. And so, he becomes responsible for taking a life on the earth plane, and through this, he (hopefully) finally learns to conquer his addiction. The next souls affected by the loss of this baby, are the parents. Perhaps the mother has chosen in her Contract, before she was born, to experience what it feels like to lose a child on the earth plane because in other lifetimes she has not valued children enough, or simply because her soul has never truly understood the human concept of "loss". So, on that deep soul level, the mother is going through her own learning and soul development. And then the father of the child – perhaps he chose before he was born to experience a life on the earth plane where he was to learn forgiveness, and the loss of his baby sends him into a complete rage where he hurts himself or another soul and must then learn to heal this and himself. Perhaps there is an older sibling of this baby who chose to learn and evolve through this loss by having to help put the pieces of his parents and his family back together again. And then the spider's web vibrates and shakes out further to affect those who created a baby car seat that was not strong enough to withstand the force of this car accident – and so they learn from this experience how to make safer and better car seats for the future. Perhaps there were those who witnessed this accident who had to learn the reality of truly living their lives in every given moment, and loving their children unconditionally, by seeing and understanding how suddenly a life can be taken. And so it goes on…. Everything happens for a reason, and in seeing the reasons we learn the lessons and we master ourselves and our soul's journey.

Often people ask me why anyone would choose to be born into a family that abuses them, beats them or neglects them. To answer this, I will take you back to my analogy of the spider web. Once again, many many people are affected by such things in this scenario: the victim, the perpetrator, the families of both the victim and the perpetrator, the child's playmates, the schools/teachers, the doctors/ hospitals, the neighbours, the Courts, the prisons, etc, etc. There can often be karmic reasons why a soul has chosen to experience such things in life. The soul who plays the role of the victim in this lifetime could well have been the perpetrator in another lifetime and is now back for karmic reasons, and also to experience the other side of the fence in order to gain a better understanding of these roles along the journey of soul knowledge and learning. The earth plane is a School of Learning because we "feel" everything so intensely here. It is only through feeling and experiencing that we can fully and completely know and understand what that situation is really all about. It's like becoming a Carpenter, for instance. You can read a million books on how to hammer in a nail but until you actually pick up that hammer in your own hand and hit that nail you have no idea what it feels like to do so. This is why, especially as children, we often have such a need to do things that we are told not to. We need to "feel" the experience to truly know and understand it.

No matter what family we chose to be born into, we will have big things to learn from the first approximately six years of being predominantly in their energy. For myself, I was born a free spirit, highly intuitive and VERY sensitive. The young me wanted to break free from all restrictions and controls put upon me, as it sought freedom from a young age. And so, I chose a mother who loved me but also had a lot of rules and was very controlling. For years we did battle with one another. When I started to learn about astrology and soul journeys I questioned Spirit as to why on earth I had chosen a mother who stopped me from developing my sensitivity and intuition, rather than helped me to do so. I was given the answer that I chose my mother because she grounded me and if I had not chosen her I would have chosen pure escapism over reality throughout my lifetime. And this answer rang true. I was not an easy child or teenager and without the structure and rules that my mother made for me, I would have been even worse.

Our early childhoods, as loving or challenging as they seem, bring us deep and ingrained lessons and experiences that we sometimess seem to spend the rest of our lives trying to relearn or rectify. Or, these experiences can make us strong and confident children who grow to be strong and confident adults. No matter what the conditions, there will always be lessons and there will always be challenges.

# CHAPTER 5

# CHOOSING YOUR LIFE

*("Are you serious – I chose what?")*

I spoke earlier of how we "choose our lives before we are born". In knowing and accepting this you take the first step towards full responsibility for your life and for yourself. The knowledge that all you have been through and all that is still to come has been pre-destined and chosen by you is a gift in itself because you can know that if you chose this, you must have done so for a very good reason. Then you can start to decipher the reason you chose a certain experience by looking to what that experience taught you and how you have changed from going through it. As you begin to do this with your past, you will find that the present and the future no longer hang over you like some pre-conceived jail sentence of unhappiness and suffering. You will slowly but surely allow yourself to start letting go of control and detaching from the emotional body through which the humanness of you views everything. The more you do this, the more peace, harmony, and joy you make room for in your life where once there was only stress and discomfort.

I will now share with you a brief insight into the process that we all go through while in the Spirit world that enables us to choose our next lifetime and all that we need and wish to go through and be, to further evolve our souls along their journey of reincarnation.

Let's assume that you have just returned to Spirit after a life on the earth plane. I would like to add here that you NEVER EVER pass over to the Spirit world on your own. Just before your time comes, your Spirit family, loved ones who have already passed over and other Angelic Beings, will come to you to reassure you, to hold your hand and take you to the other side of the veil. Depending on how you pass over at your time of death, you will need to rest for a period of time to adjust to the energy, and for some souls to adjust to the awareness that they are no longer on the earth plane. If you died suddenly, then it could take some time to adjust as there may be much sadness as to what and who you left behind, or confusion as to how you ended up dead. Or, you may have been sick for many years and so returning home to Spirit free of that pain and suffering is a wondrous and happy thing for you. Whatever your circumstances, there will be a period of rest for you, first and foremost.

Once you are rested and ready to look at what your soul needs to experience and learn next, you firstly go to a space in the Spiritual Realms called "The Hall of Mirrors". In this space, you get to see your whole life – the life you just lived on the earth plane – laid out in front of you like a movie, with you in the starring role. You get to see every person who was in your life and how you affected them as well as how they affected you. You also get to see every experience you had and what the implications and consequences of these were. You get to see all that you learned from these events and happenings, and what those around you experienced through your learning when they were a part of that experience too. As you see how you lived your life, you will be shown how the words, reactions, actions, and energy you gave out affected everyone around you as well. As you see how you were hurt, you will also see how you hurt others. As you were loved, you will see the effect of your love on others too. You watch all of this, and if there are other past lives related to what you experienced in this most recent lifetime, then these will also be shown to you. What you need to be aware of with this intimate look into your life is that all you are seeing and feeling in the Hall of Mirrors is done by you without the Ego or Lower Self. You are seeing everything through the eyes of love, compassion, and heightened understanding. When you see yourself seeking revenge for a hurt you suffered in that lifetime, you do not feel those vengeful emotions; instead you feel deep compassion and empathy for the one you sought revenge upon and for yourself for choosing to act that way. When you see yourself broken-hearted due to being betrayed by another soul on the earth plane, you can see why that betrayal had to take place and what it meant for that other soul to treat you in that way. In the energy of the Spirit World, and therefore in the Hall of Mirrors, there is only LOVE and understanding for all that your soul chose to learn and how much of what was chosen got to be fulfilled and mastered. And so you watch, you listen, and you start to make a plan for your next lifetime on the earth plane – should you wish to come back – of what you can put right, learn, experience and grow from. This plan will later become your Natal Chart or Birth Chart and all that you choose becomes reflected in the planets and signs of the zodiac, as the energies of the cosmos are your greatest tools to navigate and support your soul's journey.

In other words, after you have watched your last lifetime in the Hall of Mirrors and any other relevant lifetimes to this particular one, you start to formulate a plan and chart out the astrological support for all that you wish to do, be and experience. This plan you are creating becomes your Contract with the Spirit World for your next lifetime on the earth plane.

You look at what you need to still learn and, based on what you have recently experienced in your last lifetime on the earth plane as well as the many other lifetimes your soul may have visited here, you create your Contract. For instance, you may realise that in that lifetime you had said that you were going to learn a lot about self-worth and self-confidence, as well as serious illness. But in the circumstances that you created for yourself in that lifetime, you ran away from having to face up to and learn these things. And so, you decide that in this next lifetime you are going to come back and challenge yourself to learn these lessons once again. You are going to choose some very difficult circumstances to work through, and you are going to bring with you gifts and talents that have the power to change how you feel about yourself. You also choose to have certain other souls incarnating on the earth plane to be in your life to help you learn all of this, through conflict and through love. And so perhaps you choose to do the following life scenario:-

- You decide to be born to affluent parents who divorce and remarry new partners. You live in the same city for most of your life, go through some challenges with learning and school as a child, become involved with drugs in your teens and early twenties and become somewhat of a hermit. All of this, you brilliantly overcome and then you go on to become an incredible and famous musician. Sometime in your thirties you will develop a serious illness – survive this, and then pass over at the age of 65 from natural causes. This is the Contract you have made with Spirit for this lifetime on the earth plane. Below is how it can actually pan out once you are down here and living in the duality energy of the earth plane. *(The italic lettering represents your Soul's reasoning.)*

- At the age of 5, your parents' divorce in a way that is not fully explained to you, or that you are unable to understand. Your self-worth and confidence is challenged for the first time. *Your soul sees this as your first opportunity to learn.* The humanness of you, however, looks to what you have done wrong and blames itself.

- At the age of 8, your mother marries a new partner who does not like you or wish for you to be around. Once again you feel worthless and unloved. *Your soul sees this as another challenge that you can use to enhance your development and a challenge that you can easily overcome on the earth plane.* The humanness of you, however, feels isolated, unwanted and angry.

–   At the age of 10 you are sent to boarding school. You have a learning disability which means that you find it hard to keep up with what you are being taught. Your worth and confidence in yourself is further challenged. *Your soul truly believes that by choosing this lesson you can mature and become stronger and as you have cleverly placed a supportive teacher or two there to help you, you will be fine.* The humanness of you becomes more angry and more frustrated and will not look or ask for help as your sense of worth will not allow itself to be further rejected or judged

–   At the age of 15, you drop out of School and your parents disown you. You are forced into independence and as a way of coping you turn to drugs and alcohol. *As a soul making this choice, you fully believe that through these experiences you will see how much you have to offer as well as how much you have to lose and therefore you will evolve fully, and your life on the earth plane will then be wonderful.* The humanness of you delights in the escapism and the numbness but sinks deeper and deeper into self-pity and loss of purpose

–   At the age of 22, you spend most of your time in your room making incredible music that no-one hears. The few friends that you once knew have given up trying to help you as you simply won't allow them to. You are lost, alone and full of anger and resentment for all that you feel the world has done to you. *Your soul believes that by choosing this time on your own, surely you will then know what to do to change it around, as you have given yourself such an incredible creative talent with music and this has the ability to change everything.* The humanness of you has given up having any belief in you and any bright or successful future that you could have in this lifetime

– At the age of 28 (your Saturn Return), your physical body has been through a lot; your kidneys shut down and you become seriously ill. You end up in the hospital for an extended stay and you meet another patient whom you fall in love with. This person hears your music and sees you for the beautiful soul that you are, and for a while there is true happiness and peace in your life. *Your soul is confident that this is all that you will need in this lifetime to change your life around and find peace, happiness, and joy – because love solves everything, right?* The humanness of you revels in the validation that is coming from outside of you but does not allow these positive and inspiring energies to be fully absorbed into you, as the damage of your childhood has not been healed enough for you to fully integrate and accept your talent and beauty, or the love of another soul.

– At the age of 35, you are out of the hospital with only one kidney. Your music is fast becoming popular and profitable, and then the love of your life leaves you for another woman. *Your soul has full confidence that all that you have been through to date in this lifetime has left you fully equipped to deal with this; it is also well aware that there is someone else out there who will love you even more than this person did.* The humanness of you falls apart like a house of cards – the love that was in your life and sustaining you to date has gone and there was no back up for this energy and no Plan B

– At the age of 40 (your Uranus opposition), you are successful in society's terms but you have never felt more alone, more worthless and less able to cope with life. There is no real pleasure for you in anything that you do because after all that you have been through and experienced you still have not learned to love yourself, believe in yourself and stand tall in your own personal power. You stop listening to your Higher Self or allowing it to have any influence over you. And so, you take your own life.

Now, just to remind you once again here, you were a soul choosing this lifetime before you were born. You made all the above choices whilst standing in your Higher Self energy – the part of you that only knows love and just wants to understand and evolve to a higher vibration. You, at this stage of planning and choosing, have completely forgotten how hard life is on the earth plane. You forgot about the Pandora's box full of emotions down here, and how hard life can be, and you forgot about the power of your Ego and your free will.

Before you go on to live this life you have chosen in intricate detail, based on the loving belief that all that you will experience here can only but make you a more evolved soul and more compassionate being, you meet with a group of energies called The Lords of Karma.

It is the job of these energies to talk sense into us and to remind us of how hard it is on the earth plane, and of how heavy a burden all the choices you are making could be to bear. They are our regulators, as they want nothing more than our success, but they can also see through the "veil of forgetfulness" that we pass through as we enter into the earth plane through the physical birthing process.

In the above scenario, they try to convince you that what you are choosing is going to be very, very difficult. But as a soul, and being fully in your Higher Self energy, you believe that you can do this; all you can really see is how much you will learn from these experiences, and how much benefit they will have to your soul's journey. And so, you go ahead and choose all of the above except for (95%) of the time, one thing. It is considered extremely uncommon to ever CHOOSE suicide as part of your soul's journey in a lifetime on the earth plane.

This is usually not a choice that a soul makes as the soul ALWAYS believes it can handle the choices it makes when in Spirit form. It has only complete and utter belief in itself to succeed.

Let me make it abundantly clear to you all that there is NO judgement in Spirit for suicide. None whatsoever. All there is, is sadness for you that you did not master all those things that you chose to do because you truly believed they were going to help you to ascend. As a soul choosing your life before you were born, you had incredible faith in yourself, in your ability to conquer all challenges put in your way and that you would not fail in your quest to do all of this. The Lords of Karma tried to tell you, but you were so confident that you could do all of this. Yet once you got here, it was all just too hard to continue.

Although there is NO judgement in Spirit for suicide, there is the matter of the Contract that you agreed to complete. That is, in the above scenario, that you agreed to live on the earth plane until you were at the age of 65. And instead, you have chosen to exit the earth plane 25 years before this. Therefore, your Contract was reneged upon and you owe it 25 years.

Now, I am once again going to take you back to my analogy of the spider's web.

Your soul is now back in Spirit, you have rested, and you have visited the Hall of Mirrors once again and, stripped of earthly Ego and through the eyes of your Higher Self, you see all that you chose and all that you didn't complete in that last lifetime. However, this time around in your next incarnation on the earth plane, your choices will be based on what you can achieve, learn, accomplish, teach others as well as experience and do, in that 25 year time frame. In other words, the next life you choose will only be 25 years long.

With this in mind, your choices for your next lifetime will undoubtedly involve a lot of learning and lessons for those around you. In this next lifetime, you could choose for instance to die at the age of 25 from a rare genetic illness. A part of this will involve major learning for the medical profession, either in general or for a particular Doctor, on advancing their skills in modern medicine. Another part of your journey will involve parents who have chosen to lose a child through something inherited from one of them. Therefore, there are many lessons for the parents in not only loss, but the guilt and responsibility they may feel, and have to learn to rise above. I feel in this case, most of the lessons would be for the soul to truly love and live life to the fullest, because deep within they have the soul knowing that they are not here for a long time; their mission is to show and teach others how to make the most of every minute they are here on the earth plane.

Whilst we are in Spirit and/or living in other existences, we have only Love because we are all only Love as part of the oneness and as a part of the Universal energy. There is no duality as there is here on the earth plane. There is just Love. And it is our soul's highest calling and highest intent to be able to live in that pure Love energy here on the earth plane.

*"As above – so below"*

# CHAPTER 6

# THE EARTH PLANE – OUR SCHOOL OF LEARNING

*("We're not getting out of here alive.")*

To choose to have an incarnation on the earth plane takes incredible courage and fortitude. Many, many souls have chosen to not ever do this because, quite simply, the earth plane is Hell. Many of the Ascended Masters, whom I work so closely with, have only had one or two lifetimes on the earth plane as the intensity of learning is so extreme here that they have felt their energy is better served to the earth plane from above. However, the very fact that they had incarnations here gives them the insight and understanding needed to guide us and take care of all who have chosen to have the "human experience". Contrary to what many religions would have you believe, there is no terrible place called "Hell" that we go to when we pass over. We don't burn in damnation for the choices we made in our lives, we don't suffer for all eternity because we chose to break society's laws on the earth plane, and we are certainly not cursed for the perceived "mistakes" we made in our lives here.

The earth plane is Hell because it is only here, on this plane of existence, that we experience the full extent of human emotions. There are basically only two emotions on the earth plane: Love and Fear. Love is what our Higher Self and soul resonate entirely with. Fear, on the other hand, contains every negative human emotion you can imagine: envy, hatred, judgement, bias, bigotry, greed, negativity, abuse, violence, intolerance and so on. As Spirit having the human experience, it is through these negative and challenging emotions that we learn the most.

To be honest, the humanness of us can be pretty stupid as it tends to only learn the hard way. Time and time again in your life you are presented with easy and loving ways to solve your problems and face your challenges, but time and time again you choose the hard way. For instance, we can surround ourselves with people who tell us how wonderful we are and how worthwhile we are, yet this can have no impact on us at all on that inner level of self-love and self-worth. But when we are constantly put down, told we are not good enough, or made to feel less than the perfect God-spark that we are, we learn, the hard way, to stand up for ourselves and for who we truly are. We start to evolve and embrace self-love and self-worth – which are our inner batteries and power houses.

We live in societies, for the most part, where how we look, what we do and how much we earn dictates our "success" in life. Social media, the News, Magazines and Newspapers, Movies and TV series – they all dictate to us what success looks like and what is acceptable, and so we strive and struggle to fit into that box. Society does not judge us as being successful just because we have found peace and happiness in our lives. Oh no, that is just brushed over by our Egos as being an insignificant accomplishment or not even fit to feature. I would challenge any of you reading this who have found inner peace on any level to say that it has not brought you more, or even the most, happiness and joy in your life. And truly, if you are in a space of happiness, peace, and joy then how can you not be successful at everything else around you and in everything you do? We are not encouraged to understand that our free will is the biggest asset we have. Instead, we allow our free will to dictate to us in terms that are not for our highest good, or for the highest good of this planet. We are controlled, indoctrinated and made to believe that only by following society's rules can we ever be accepted, let alone be successful in life.

We make it so hard to find happiness when we allow ourselves to be constantly conditioned and judged by what society tells us. It is really not until we let go of this judgement dis-ease that we can allow ourselves to see our own unique beauty and magnificence through being who we truly are.

*"There is nothing wrong with you and you have done nothing wrong – you are just a soul on a journey of learning through your life experiences"*

Once we have been through the Hall of Mirrors and decided what it is we wish to learn, experience and be in our next lifetime we then choose our time, date and place of birth, with the assistance of the finest Spiritual Astrologers. The planets have to be in definite signs of the zodiac and be forming particular aspects to one another for the experiences that we need to learn from to create themselves, and for us to receive the planetary support that we need to get through. Our mental, emotional, spiritual and physical bodies need to be aligned in the best way possible for us to learn what we have chosen to from this life on the earth plane. All of these pre-chosen alignments and placements create our Natal Chart, and this then becomes the map that we must follow throughout a lifetime down here. This is the very crux of it all – the Natal Chart is, and always will be, the most honest, in-depth and informative guide you will ever need for navigating your existence on the earth plane. We are not meant to be here walking blindly; it doesn't have to be that hard. There is a perfect guide and tool that you yourself chose before you were born - your Natal Chart. So why would you not want to discover and decipher this?

The sign of the zodiac that we choose to be born under, our Sun sign, is the primary focus and therefore defines our inner self and the inner basis from which we will learn. Each sign of the zodiac has specific lessons associated with it, both on a practical level and on a spiritual level. We are made up of all the planets and all the signs of the zodiac but not in equal amounts. For instance, you could be born in the water sign of Pisces, but most of your other planets sit in earth signs such as Taurus or in fire signs such as Leo. So, although the Piscean Sun is your primary focus, the abundance of planets in other signs have important and significant influences over how you go about living your life, how you react in certain situations, and what experiences you will embrace or run from. Even if all of your planets are sitting in Earth signs, and only your Sun is in Pisces, you are still going to be sensitive, creative and imaginative in some way. At the end of the day, it is always good to remember that it is your Sun that is who you truly are, and the energies of your Sun sign are the ones you are here to learn to use in a constructive and productive way, rather than in a destructive and pointless way. The greatest challenge for all of us, whether we are aware of it or not, is that we try to run away from our Sun sign. We try to hide from the more challenging or negative qualities that sign may possess. With a bit more knowledge of your astrological make-up, you can see how to manipulate and make use of these qualities rather than hide from them, disregard them or treat them as negative.

For instance, let's take the Sun sign of Virgo – renowned for its need for perfection, having everything in place and desiring to be in control and managing everything. This type of energy and way of being is ideal in the work place and especially good for any job/career that requires attention to detail, management skills, and a perfectionistic attitude. It creates the "perfect" employee who can always be relied upon to take care of business. However, this type of energy in your personal life means that you can be controlling of others and their choices, you can never be satisfied with your life, how you look and what you do, as you always feel like you are not "perfect" enough. You can't just relax and go with the flow, and so your life is a constant struggle.

Therefore, there really are no negative qualities to any sign of the zodiac, rather there are challenges and opportunities to change the energy and make it what you need it to be, make it your friend, rather than feeling that you must eradicate it or fight against it.

# Esoteric Astrology House System

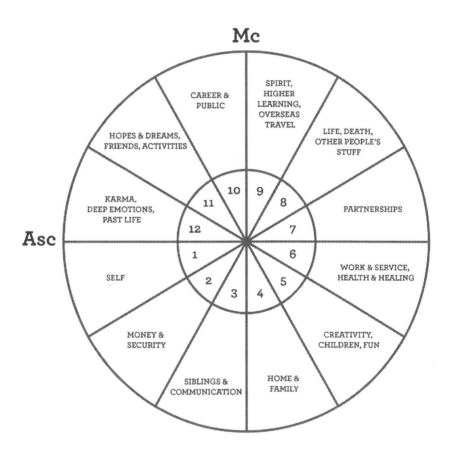

| **HOUSE 1** | **SELF** |
| | How you feel about yourself. Your physical structure and character |

| **HOUSE 2** | **MONEY & SECURITY** |
| | Money you earn. What determines security and safety in your life |

| **HOUSE 3** | **COMMUNICATION & SIBLINGS** |
| | How you communicate, read, listen and learn. Your relationship with your brothers and sisters. Short distance travel. Real Estate. |

| **HOUSE 4** | **HOME & FAMILY** |
| | Your upbringing and the home you grew up in. The home and family you create for yourself. |

| **HOUSE 5** | **CREATIVITY, CHILDREN, FUN** |
| | Your creative talents. Your relationship with children (your own and others). Fun, romance, sport. |

| **HOUSE 6** | **HEALTH & HEALING AND WORK & SERVICE** |
| | Your daily work and daily life. Your health. Your ability to heal. |

| **HOUSE 7** | **PARTNERSHIPS** |
| | Marriages. Business partnerships. Legal contracts. |

| **HOUSE 8** | **LIFE, DEATH, OTHER PEOPLE'S STUFF** |
| | Inheritances, taxes, shared resources, sex, metaphysics, control, transformation. |

| **HOUSE 9** | **SPIRIT, OVERSEAS TRAVEL, HIGHER LEARNING** |
| | Your spirituality. Overseas travel and foreign interests. Learning that you choose to do, rather than what you have to do. |

| **HOUSE 10** | **CAREER & PUBLIC** |
| | Your career. What you do in the public eye. |

| **HOUSE 11** | **HOPES, WISHES & DREAMS AND FRIENDS & SOCIAL ACTIVITIES** |
| | Your dreams and goals for the future. Friends, teams, committees, social networks. |

| **HOUSE 12** | **KARMA, PAST LIFE ENERGY, DEEP EMOTIONS** |
| | All that affects you emotionally, but is hidden from view and is buried within you and how you deal with this |

| **ASC** | **ASCENDANT** |
| | How you present yourself to the world - the outer you |

| **MC** | **MID-HEAVEN** |
| | How you naturally think. Your destiny in this lifetime |

# Natal Chart

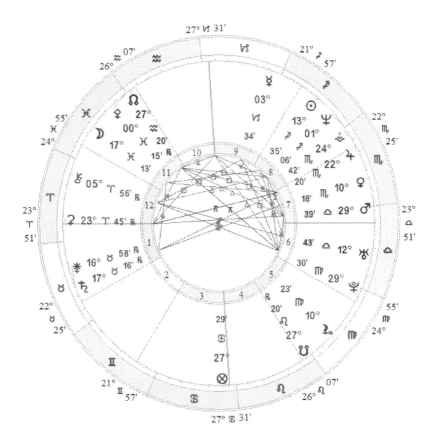

# CHAPTER 7

# YOUR NATAL CHART – YOUR BLUE PRINT

*("But wait…there's a Plan!")*

I cannot express enough the importance of knowing your Natal Chart. Many spiritual teachers have echoed this around the world since the beginning of time. Without this knowledge you are blind to what your life is all about. All that you chose and therefore everything you experience can only be evaluated by you from an emotional or human perspective, as you are ignorant of the true picture. Life on the earth plane is a challenge; there is no doubt about that. But when you know and understand your strengths, weaknesses, gifts and talents, you are no longer blind – you can instead join the dots, fill in the jigsaw pieces and live your life, rather than existing and bouncing around from experience to experience with no idea where you are going or what it is all about.

For so long as you are 'travelling blind" in this lifetime you are unaware of the bigger picture and often completely at the mercy of all that life makes you "feel". Therefore, you often feel the need to change or to control those that come into your life, as only what you can see, and feel is real to you. Everyone who is in your life is there for a reason – you put them there and chose them to be your teachers in this lifetime just the way they are. You cannot change another soul and it is never right to try to do so. What you can change and have complete power and permission to do so, is yourself. You can change the way you see things, the way you react to things and most importantly the way you deal with things. In doing this, you send out an energy to those around whom you feel need to change. By watching you and being in your energy they can then make the decision or choice to change their ways; they can evolve and grow through their relationship with you – whatever that relationship may be.

Often there are those in your life whom you can see making the same mistakes over and over again and the compassion and empathy within you just wants to reach out and rescue them or help them in some way. However, these perceived "mistakes" that they are making in their lives are their learning. If you rescue them from the experience or help them out every time they get in trouble, you are actually doing them a disservice. By overly involving yourself in their lives, you are doing their learning for them and therefore stopping them from achieving what they have chosen to come here to learn and to be. And so they keep repeating those mistakes, and learn nothing from life as that breakdown, loss or confusion they are feeling is what they are here to work through, not you. We are here to support one another and to offer each other guidance and advice, not to live their lives for them. The other aspect of overly involving yourself in the life challenges of others is that in doing this you are also taking your attention away from what you yourself need to learn and work upon along your life journey.

The image I am given for this is the one of a person stuck down a deep well. At the bottom of that well it is dark and lonely, but when they look up there is a light there. You want to help this person, but you are of no use whatsoever to that person if you jump in the well with them, as then you are both stuck down there, unable to get out and unable to help one another; all you can do is suffer together. And, if you go down that well, throw them over your shoulder and carry them out, you are also of no real or sustainable use to them, as although they may be now out of the well, they have no learning or know-how of how to get out of there by themselves. In both of these scenarios you are not allowing the person stuck there to learn anything from the experience, and so inevitably they will find themselves there once again.

However, if you were to stand at the top of the Well and throw down a rope ladder that they can hang on to, start to climb and use to lift themselves up, you are giving them the help they need with no danger to you. Every step they take up that ladder to get out of the deep dark well is of their own doing and with every step taken they learn something new. They learn to support themselves, rescue themselves and believe in themselves as a result.

It is always important to remember that you cannot change another soul – you can only change yourself. The power you have to live and love your life is for you alone. When you use this power to change yourself, your perceptions and the way you live your life, you set an example to others as well as become a guide who can help others to make their own necessary changes. So often in life, people, women especially, go into relationships where they try to change that partner from the person they were initially attracted to into someone that they feel will be a better version. More often than not, that very thing that so attracted you to a person in the first place is the thing you try to change, or what you end up resenting about them in the long run. Always look to the learning – always look to what is happening in your relationships and your life that goes beyond what it initially makes you feel. For so long as you live your life entrapped by what you feel rather than what you are learning, you are treading water and neither floating nor swimming. That need to change another person is often a reflection back to you, of what you don't like about yourself or what you need to change in yourself. And often the only change that is needed is your perspective – so simple yet so hard when we are stuck in our Ego selves.

# CHAPTER 8

# THE SUN SIGNS

*("What's really lurking underneath.")*

We are made up of all 12 signs of the zodiac as well as all the planets in our Solar System. From an esoteric astrology perspective, we can look at the five most important planets and placements that define who you are, and what your soul's journey through this lifetime is all about. The first placement, and the only one you can be sure to know without having to consult your Natal Chart is your Sun, defined by your date of birth. The Sun is your primary focus in life and the sign of the zodiac that it sits in shows you how you are to learn and evolve through using the energy of this sign to identify and align with who you truly are. Your Sun is considered to be your reality and your presence on the earth plane. Once upon a time, it was the Moon sign that everyone knew of first in their astrology, but since the world swayed towards the patriarchal ways rather than the matriarchal ways, it is now the Sun that we are directed to look too first.

The following is a list of all the Sun signs and what it can mean and feel for you to be born under each sign. Your Sun sign shows what comes naturally to you and how your responses and reactions to life are processed by you on that inner and instinctual "human" level. After each sign, written in bold, is the esoteric and spiritual lesson associated with that particular Sun sign.

## SUN IN ARIES

Aries is the first sign of the zodiac and therefore all souls born under this sign have varying degrees of the need to come first and to be the leader. Many Arian children born into families, and not as the first-born child, can have friction with older siblings, as underneath it all they believe they come first even though they are younger. They will fight with their older siblings simply because they feel they are not in the position they should be. Their passionate, headstrong and determined way of being is determined not to be ignored or relegated in any way.

Being the first sign of the zodiac, no-one has a stronger will or more determination to get their way and to make things happen. Arians are headstrong and strong-willed, and demand to have their own way. They are natural leaders and will happily rush in where others fear to tread – but sometimes it's all about the rush, the pursuit and the chase, and not a lot else.

At their absolute best, Arian souls are inspirational leaders who can champion the way for others, forge ahead where others stand in fear and bring much determination and forthrightness to any situation. These are the qualities that they can develop productively to use in their careers, to get ahead and achieve success and status. Aries is ruled by the planet of passion and war, Mars. The challenge for them is to keep going and keep the interest when the initial thrill of the chase or challenge is over. If they cannot keep that momentum going, they can go to the other extreme and do nothing. It's all or nothing with an Arian soul and they need action to feel and be at their best. An unemployed or unmotivated Arian is not a happy person and so it is their challenge to find that action and motivation in all aspects of what they do, rather than only applying themselves to their own single-minded pursuits.

**Souls born with the Sun in Aries tend to look at life through a black and white lens. Therefore, it is their greatest life lesson to learn to explore the grey or coloured areas in life, as this is where their true learning lies.**

## SUN IN TAURUS

Taurus is the second sign of the zodiac and so we move from action to pause - or the need to hold on to what we have begun so it can be our safety and our security.

Taurean souls approach life and live their lives in a methodical, grounded and cautious manner. For the most part, they like things to stay the same in life as this way they feel secure and unthreatened. They like to surround themselves with the finer things in life (being ruled by Venus); although they often prefer such things to be luxurious and expensive, as long as they are beautiful, comfortable and cherished Taureans will be happy in that energy. Taurus the Bull does not like change, particularly so if someone else is instigating it. It's difficult to make Taureans do anything they do not want to do, and even when they do it, it will be in their own time and in their own way. So, the key to getting what you want out of a Taurean soul is to teach them to compromise and meet you halfway. Taureans are very sensitive souls too and easily hurt by the words and actions of others. Unfortunately, their typical "go to" in such situations, is to sulk, refuse to communicate their feelings and to stay stuck in their pain and suffering. They are at their happiest when they can use their hands to create – whether this be cooking, painting or gardening. They love to immerse themselves in what is natural and to create from that ground level. However, they can be lazy, and allow themselves to become stuck in what they are feeling emotionally, which stops them from taking any action at all. They will sit on the couch, eat chocolate and feel hard done by until such a time as they feel good and ready to move on. Moving on from a problem for a Taurus does not mean letting go of the issue; these souls can hold a grudge longer than any other sign of the zodiac.

**These souls often live by the motto "never forgive and never forget". Their greatest life lesson is to learn to forgive so they can find the true peace that they crave in the present moment, and to let themselves and others off the hook.**

## SUN IN GEMINI

For those born a Gemini, there is much mental activity. They are always thinking, planning and analysing. They are "ideas" people, with huge imaginations, a penchant for fun and a craving for stimulation and variety in all that they do. To this end, Gemini souls can find it exceedingly difficult to finish anything that they start. They are the instigators of the zodiac. As the first Air sign of the zodiac, it is, for them, all about what goes on in the head and not enough about following that through to fruition. This can create a journey of self-sabotage throughout their lifetimes, especially if they are not taught to follow things through to completion as children. Gemini women are the most capable and competent women of the zodiac as they have an attitude of "can do". They will give anything a try, and if it doesn't work out, then they can happily leave it to one side and move on to the next challenge. This is one of the true gifts of Gemini - the ability to take on new things with ease. The lightness and brightness of this air sign can have you tricked and trumped from all aspects, and it is no surprise that Gemini is ruled by Mercury, the messenger of the Gods. These souls are good at reading situations, and to this end specialise in telling people what THEY think you need to hear, which more often than not is a shade of the truth but not the whole true story. The importance of deep and complete honesty is terrifying for these souls as it means they must reveal parts of themselves that they would rather not know about.

Such things pull them down from that airy carefree energy to deeper than ground level reality, and they do not like this one little bit.

**The greatest life lesson for a Gemini is to learn to put thoughts into action and to go deeper within to acknowledge and accept the soul they really are, without covering it up with social chatter, entertaining stories, and miscellaneous actions.**

## SUN IN CANCER

With a Cancerian Sun, one is more often than not born with a lack of self-love and a lack of self-worth, and this can come with a strong sense of guilt – a feeling that you have done something wrong and that you are not worthy of love. This is sometimes known as *"the energy of the Fallen Angel"*. This is the first water sign of the zodiac and is ruled by the Moon, therefore the first powerful flow of emotions begins here. Most Cancerians are born psychic. The water signs tend to "feel" this energy within them. As water is a natural conduit for spiritual energy, the knowings and feelings that they have intuitively flow through them and out of them to heal and nurture others. Cancerians are often what is known as "emotional clearing houses". They absorb the negative energy from those around them – whether that be family members or someone in the supermarket – as part of the healing contract they have with the Spirit world. Cancerian souls choose, before they are born, to do this work for Spirit on the earth plane and therefore it is imperative that they also know how to protect themselves from negative energy and how to clear themselves of it as well. The moodiness that they are so renowned for is often caused by what they absorb from others and then feel and own as their own. Cancerians are born with a need to take care of others, especially those who cannot take care of themselves. They feel that the more needed they are by others, the better a person they must be. However, in their need to take care of everyone around them, they forget about themselves; they do not nurture, love or nourish themselves as the needs of everyone else are always more important. While running around through their lives working at being everything to everyone, they start to realise that this energy is not reciprocated. Bitterness and resentment can build, and what they once did with love and compassion becomes a chore and something they do not wish to be a part of. Yet the guilt holds them there.

**The major life lesson for a Cancerian soul is to learn self-love and self-worth and to validate herself/himself for all that they are, so as their cup is always full and the love that others bring to them just causes it to overflow.**

## SUN IN LEO

Souls born with the Sun in Leo are courageous and outgoing, and they love to be admired for all that they bring to the table. They have huge hearts; they would do anything for anyone. Their greatest motivation is to shine and to be seen – so no surprises in how many Movie Stars and Rock Stars are Leos! Leo is the second Fire sign and is ruled by the Sun. As the Arian leads with the steadfast surety that it is his way or the highway, the Leo leads with love and compassion, so as others truly want to follow them and believe in them. The Leo soul is dramatic and creative and great fun to be around. They are here to learn and understand that what they go after in life needs more energy put into it than just the chase. The willpower and tenacity they put into the chase, can also be brought through to complete the kill (in Lion talk). Their challenge is always to make that follow through complete by learning to align what is for the highest good (theirs and that of all concerned) with the action they are taking. That feeling of being the King of the Jungle is strong within them, but humility and awareness of others are also needed if they are to achieve the highest and best results for all concerned. Pride comes before a fall, and most Leos will have to experience such a thing in their lifetime in order to understand who they truly are and how to successfully align the very best they can be with the highest needs of all involved.

**The greatest life lesson for a Leo soul is to learn to do things in life because they are the right thing to do, and not for the glory or kudos such things may bring to them.**

## SUN IN VIRGO

When you are born with your Sun in Virgo you are born a perfectionist in some or many ways. For some Virgos, this energy goes through into every aspect of their lives; for others, it is only in specific areas. These souls have an amazing ability to heal because they themselves arrive here feeling wounded and so in need of healing – hence the search for perfection, as they believe only through achieving this can they be the perfect soul that they expect themselves to be, as then the hurting will stop. Therefore, it makes perfect sense to Esoteric Astrologers that the planet Chiron rules Virgo. If you are born a Virgo you are born doing and giving your best. The only exception to this is if the fear of failure, or of not being the best, becomes so much that you won't even try. (We all have Virgo energy somewhere in our Natal Charts and this is where we personally seek perfection or have a huge fear of failure). More than anything, a Virgo needs to be perceived by others as being capable and competent of all that is asked of them and so they are capable of putting incredible pressure and stress on themselves to achieve ridiculous standards and unachievable heights. This is not the Air sign huge imagination type of belief, this is hard-working, task bearing, load carrying energy that no soul should ever put upon themselves. Learning to be kind and gentle with themself no matter what the situation is, and to be able to accept themself whatever their gifts or limits may be, can be a lifetime work in progress for a Virgo. However, along the way they can be the most valued and sought after employees any business could ask for.

**The Virgo soul is here to learn that doing their best is the only perfection that there is and to see this within themself as others see it in them.**

## SUN IN LIBRA

To be born with the Sun in Libra is to be born the "people pleaser". The need for harmony and balance is so strong that they will often go along with others even when it is not what they want, and can often appear to be quite shallow as a result of this. They are here to not only learn about balance but to create it in their life in every way. Rather than doing so by going with the flow, they are here to differentiate and learn about balance by being assertive and putting themselves forward as well. Libran souls have an amazing ability to be able to see both sides of any story, and therefore they make good counsellors, teachers, negotiators, and mediators. Ruled by a combination of Mercury and Venus they embrace communication and all that is beautiful in life. Their need for balance is easily applied to their work and careers where they find it easy to speak up and step up. In their personal lives, however, this can be much more of a challenge. For instance, Librans are notorious for not being able to make up their minds and make choices in life. This is because when given the power to choose, their default is more often than not "what do you want?" Rather than upset the apple cart by expressing what they want, which possibly is NOT what everybody else wants, they hand over their responsibility to others, and in doing so they take away their own personal power and end up not getting what they want. Similar to the Cancerian, the need to please others is strong in these souls. But as Cancerians do it to make themselves feel better, Librans do it because they believe it will keep the peace. Libran souls tend to be very social and often do not like to be on their own. That need for balance in their lives even extends so far as to constantly needing to feel the presence of others around them.

**The greatest life lesson for the soul born under the sign of Libra is to learn to find balance in life in all that they do, and to not be afraid to stick up for themself and speak up for what they want, to achieve this.**

## SUN IN SCORPIO

Souls born with the Sun in Scorpio are the most intensely sensitive of all the star signs. Scorpio souls judge everything by how it makes them "feel" as this is their natural way of processing what is going on around them. In doing so they can be very reactive. To this end, they are renowned for their "sting" as once they are hurt it is their natural instinct to hurt back. Scorpio souls also have a great need for personal power in life, which is interesting for souls who also like to play the victim. Their need for power needs to be answered, as this is where they can really shine. However, this power is really only suitable and acceptable to others when it is used within the work place and not in their personal lives. No-one enjoys someone else lording power over them. Within the work place this can be channelled and used constructively, whereas in the family or in personal life it is a lot less acceptable. The planet Pluto rules Scorpio and supports its intensity and need to go deep. Scorpios have such fear of being hurt that they tend to like to keep secrets and play their cards close to their chest. As children, they can often feel like all attention is on them, whether they want it to be or not. They tend to want to hide things, keep things secret so they can still feel that they have some power over their inner worlds. Souls with the Sun in Scorpio can run from responsibility in their lives as they fear being judged for getting it wrong. The sooner they learn to take responsibility for all that they put their name to or energy into, the sooner they can learn to use their power constructively and step into positions of leadership and authority. They are very intuitive, but they can allow their deep penetrating minds to overlook what they intuitively feel as they seek answers through proof and research. Sensitivity is their greatest asset, and their greatest downfall until they learn to channel this creatively and/or use it to understand situations rather than judge them.

**The greatest life lesson for a Scorpio is to learn to stop and process what is being said and done BEFORE they react to it. This way it will not be a knee-jerk reaction, but rather an informed, less emotional and more realistic reaction instead.**

## SUN IN SAGITTARIUS

If you are born with your Sun in Sagittarius you tend to love freedom and hate to be controlled in any way - however, you can be controlling and judgemental of others. Sagittarian souls love adventure, excitement, fun, and variety in life. As they are ruled by the planet Jupiter they embrace all that allows them to grow and expand in life. They are extremely social and inclined to be happier having a wide circle of friends rather than a small intimate one. Sagittarians tend to be intelligent souls who choose to educate themselves thoroughly and completely in what they wish to master. Similar to Gemini (even though they are astrological opposites) they crave variety and stimulation in their lives. The difference is that Sagittarians will go on to master what they do, while Geminis often remain the "jack of all trades and the master of none". Sagittarians tend to go through life having many different jobs and careers, but everything they do will always be done well and to their highest abilities before they move on to the next project. Because they educate themselves well in their chosen field, Sagittarians are known to hold themselves above others and look down upon anyone who has not done the same amount of learning or reached the same position of power in life. They tend to be honest, however they can lack tact and often the simple filters, that can change what they say from a brutal fact to an honest opinion, just don't get activated in time. They are generous and courageous and bring a big dose of fun to any event that they are invited to, but sometimes excess and taking things too far become their worst enemy and biggest regret.

**The greatest life lesson for a Sagittarian is to learn to treat others as they themselves wish to be treated. This means to let go of controlling others and judging others, as neither of these ways are ones that they wish others to put upon them.**


## SUN IN CAPRICORN

With the Sun in Capricorn, you are the most stubborn and ambitious sign of the zodiac. Capricorn souls often go through life with their blinkers on – looking straight ahead and focussing only on the task at hand. Ruled by Saturn, this sign will always take life more seriously than any other sign of the zodiac as they truly believe that hard work, discipline and focus are the most important things in life to concentrate on. To this end, a Capricorn will ALWAYS get where they need to go in life just so long as there is a plan. These souls do not "wing it" with ease, or even like to be spontaneous or carefree. They are at their happiest when there is structure and a plan to work towards, and no-one will work harder than they do to get there. All of this seriousness though can result in them easily seeing the negative in themselves and in what is going on around them. The more they learn to take the pressure off themselves and to have fun with life, the easier life becomes for them. The other challenge that comes with all this seriousness is a lack of trust in themselves and in the world around them. Capricorn energy is often the energy of the warrior, the person who will always get things done and can be relied upon to take care of the needs of others. However, it's as if the more they feel they have to constantly take care of business, the harder they find it to trust in anything or anyone. Just allowing life to move of its own accord and go with it is the last thing a Capricorn will ever feel comfortable with, as they have a deep seeded distrust for anything that is not set in stone. And so, they hold themselves back from adventure, from experimenting with new things and often from love. Emotional trust is a huge learning curve for Capricorns and so they can have as much doubt and mistrust of the feelings of others as they do for their own feelings, simply because such things are not set in concrete and cannot be solidly presented.

**The greatest life lesson for a Capricorn is to learn to trust in the process of life – to let go - and most importantly to learn to trust in themself, their feelings and their abilities.**

## SUN IN AQUARIUS

When you are born with the Sun in Aquarius you are a free spirit, a powerful humanitarian and you are here to change the world. You see the world differently to others and you negotiate it in an alternative manner too. You dance to your own drum beat and so you are born feeling like you are different to everyone else. Ruled by the planet of change, Uranus, they are unique and innovative thinkers. Aquarians usually know and understand that they are loved and are part of a family etc, but they can still feel very much like they are on the outside looking in. They love to observe and watch the world go by, but they often hold themselves back from fully participating for fear of not being the same as everyone else or not doing things the same as everyone else. It can be easy for Aquarians to slip into depression, particularly Aquarian men, as this feeling of not quite fitting in can be hard work for the more sensitive souls out there. The most powerful thing they can do is embrace their differences, their quirkiness, their unique way of thinking, dressing and being, and share it with the world. These souls are often inventors and innovators who are able to use their intellect to communicate different ways of being and solving problems. However, being progressive and open-minded can be limited to only certain areas of their lives, while in other areas they can be conservative and stuck in their ways. One of the most powerful tools an Aquarian possesses is the ability to detach from emotional situations and drama. This detachment is what we all are here to learn as evolving souls and Aquarians have a bit of a head start on the rest of us. The more they can use this to advance themselves and teach others, the more they will change the world as they are destined to. Interestingly, although Aquarians are here to change the world, their greatest personal fear is often change itself, and they can really struggle with this, especially when someone else moves the goal posts.

**An Aquarian's greatest lesson is to learn to enjoy how different they are from others, to share their uniqueness with the world and to embrace change in life as being their personal road to success.**

## SUN IN PISCES

Souls born with the Sun in Pisces tend to be talented and connected to Spirit. Pisces is ruled by Neptune that thrives on imagination and illusion. This is the final sign of the zodiac and therefore the one that has the whole of humanity as a collection as its feet. Pisceans are usually huge humanitarians and it is often part of their life purpose in coming here to make a difference on the earth plane, especially in the way that we treat one another and the planet that we live on. These souls tend to be extremely talented in some way, and more often than not it is a creative talent. However, they lack ambition and the drive to do anything with their talents. They can be complete "fence sitters", and so just allow the world to pass them by and do not push themselves to do anything with their lives or use the incredible talents they have. It is usually not until you back a Piscean into a corner that you will get any strong reaction from them, and when this happens LOOK OUT! In general, souls born under this sign are intuitive and born Mediums. It is more normal for a Piscean soul to see, hear or feel Spirit than any other sign of the zodiac, and so it is no surprise that as children they are the ones with their heads in the clouds, happily day-dreaming in their own little worlds. The world a Piscean can create in their head is often far preferable to the world that they are living in, so it's more fun and a good escape from reality for them to just opt out every now and then and escape to where things are always good, kind and beautiful. The challenge here is that it is very easy for a Pisces to seek escapism through drugs, alcohol, television or any other vehicle that takes them away from the here and now. Pisceans are so very sensitive but, rather than feel hurt personally by what happens, they tend to feel hurt for the big picture and for everything that is going on, and that is a huge load to carry. Using tools such as meditation, and physically doing things to make a difference rather than just thinking about it and meaning to, are great ways for a Piscean to learn to escape constructively and to make the best use of their higher wisdom and knowledge.

**A Piscean's greatest life lesson is to learn to get off the fence and chase their ambitions so they can offer the best of themself to the world, and be the best that they can be.**

Now that we have established the "inner you" and what makes you tick underneath it all, you can start to get a "feel" for who you are and the essence of you. Your primary focus in this lifetime is to work with the energy of your Sun sign, to shine light on this area of your life and how you naturally feel and react here. You are learning through another lifetime on the earth plane, how it actually feels to see life and experience life through your chosen astrological lens. This forms the basis of your view and all the other planets and signs of the zodiac do their dance alongside - opposite, harmoniously, positively and/ or negatively - with your Sun, and with one another. And all of this comes together to form YOU – having this human experience at this particular time - and what you are here to learn this time around.

## CHAPTER 9

# THE ASCENDANT OR RISING SIGN

*("Playing Hide and Seek.")*

As your Sun represents the "inner you" and your primary focus in this lifetime, your Ascendant or Rising Sign represents the "outer you" or the part of you that you present to the world. This is the sign that was rising over the horizon at the time of your birth; it is the start of you, your first exposure to the world that you have chosen to live this life in. It can be your mask, the façade you hide behind, whilst the Sun and the 1st House *(see Esoteric House System diagram pages 32 and 33)* tell you who is really underneath. Your Ascendant has the ability to support you, as it is like a default to the "other half of you" when times get tough for the "inner you". This is the face that you show to the world, the external you that values highly how it is perceived by others.

As children we are often more like our Ascendants, as it is easier to display the outer part of us; we are more comfortable with it because we have not, as yet, explored our inner world. People who meet me for the first time often expect me to be able to instantly pick what star sign they are because I am an Astrologer. But as I am sure you will know by reading what you have read so far in this book, we are not just our Sun sign. We are made up of all 12 planets and all 12 signs of the zodiac and they all have relevance and they all shape us into the humanness that we experience on the earth plane.

So, your Ascendant is really the other half of you. It is how you naturally express yourself. Many people feel a lot more comfortable in their Ascendant energy than they do in their Sun energy. But it is important to know and remember that it is your Sun that was your primary choice and it is this aspect of you that you are here to learn the most from. Running from your Sun because it's easier to be your Ascendant would be like a sensitive Scorpio pretending to be a roaring Leo. It is an easier way to present yourself to the world when you don't want to show your feelings, but through being what you are not you are limiting your learning and your soul's evolution.

The following is a list of the 12 zodiac signs as Ascendants, how they shape you in the way that you express and present yourself to the world, and how you wish others to see you.

## ARIES ASCENDANT

You present yourself to the world as a natural leader. Often, no matter what job you have, or what activity you involve yourself in, you find your way to the top and into that leadership position. When you are upset, and that fire energy ignites within you, it can be hard for you to back down and you often railroad others in your determination to get your way. Learning to listen as well as you can lead is necessary for you to become the type of leader others are happy to follow.

## TAURUS ASCENDANT

You present yourself to the world as being gentle, sweet and sensitive and you have a need to feel and give affection to others. You are, however, extremely stubborn and will dig your heels in especially when it comes to anything that you feel you do not wish to do, or that has hurt you. You work at your own pace and often cannot see the difference between working too hard and not working at all.

## GEMINI ASCENDANT

You present yourself to the world as a social, easy-going and fun-loving character. You encourage others to keep it light and to be active. You have a great need to be liked and how others, especially the general public, perceive you is important to you. Your challenge here is to ground yourself and open yourself up to more depth and honesty without fear of being judged.

## CANCER ASCENDANT

You present yourself to the world as the gentle, creative and nurturing type. Others are attracted to you as you come across as being a great listener and counsellor, and so, whether you like it or not, others are going to dump their "stuff" on you a lot! You seek validation from others and love to be needed. You can become moody and emotional when you feel unloved or insecure in relationships.

## LEO ASCENDANT

You present yourself to the world with strength and confidence. You have the powerful ability to 'fake it till you make it" and this allows you to easily push through any self-confidence or self-worth issues you may have. You have a great need to be admired and will constantly put yourself out there in the public arena to collect on the kudos. You are a natural leader and others often look to you for direction or their next step.

## VIRGO ASCENDANT

You wish for everyone to perceive you as being "perfect". You pay attention to detail and can always be relied upon to take care of business. It is very important to you that others see you as competent, capable and someone that they can rely on to take care of things. You put a lot of pressure on yourself to perform in the eyes of the world and can be extremely hard on yourself and have high expectations of others. You may often have a great fear of failure.

## LIBRA ASCENDANT

You present yourself to the world as someone who is happy to go with the flow, easy-going, warm and friendly. You often hold yourself back from stating your opinions and preferences unless asked. You do this to make sure that there is always harmony, and also so you can be seen as the one that everyone likes and gets along with. This can cause others to perceive you as being somewhat shallow and easily manipulated. Due to this you can be overlooked and even walked over by others, as they just see a charming easy-going soul who will always go along with things.

## SCORPIO ASCENDANT

You give off (especially if you are a woman) a strong sexual energy that is appealing to others. Therefore, men and women are attracted to you, whether you want their attention or not. It is important that you establish firm boundaries as to what is acceptable to you and what is not. You throw yourself wholeheartedly into anything you represent and are prepared to work hard to achieve success and status in life. You come across as friendly and easy to get along with, and you are for the most part. It is not until somebody crosses you that they see how extremely sensitive you are, and how ruthlessly you can retaliate.

## SAGITTARIAN ASCENDANT

You present yourself to the world as a celebrant of fun and adventure. You love to be at the centre of the action and you are an instigator and leader rather than a follower. You are an incredible optimist and are at your happiest when you have something new to aspire to or achieve, but you can also gloss over and hide your problems and insecurities rather than worry anyone else with them. You may go along with a new venture for just so long as it pleases you, and when the lustre wears off or you lose some of your control there, you are capable of just switching off and moving on.

## CAPRICORN ASCENDANT

You present yourself to the world as someone practical, serious and someone who is more than capable of taking care of the details and the hard work necessary. You sometimes seem a little more distant and cool than others. Souls born with this Ascendant often feel like they are on a "mission" all their lives to achieve something, as their unconscious and conscious ambitions are such a driving force within them. They have a lot of learning to do regarding worrying about things that they cannot control – especially things such as the future. The challenge is to find that mission and, instead of cautiously stepping around it and not trusting in it, grab hold of it and use that Capricorn tenacity to make it a reality.

## AQUARIUS ASCENDANT

You present yourself to the world as someone who is quirky, outside the box and who dances to their own drumbeat. You often feel like you don't fit in with those around you and can be judgemental of yourself and how others perceive you. You love to observe the world around you, often rather than participating in it. How you appear to others may be a complete contradiction to how you view yourself.

You must learn to make peace with who you are and enjoy everything about you that makes you so very unique and special. You easily attract others to you, as you are so open to new ideas and anything that challenges you to think innovatively and outside of the box.

## PISCES ASCENDANT

You present yourself to the world as easy-going and gentle whilst underneath there can be so much worry and anxiety going on. You feel that pull to the Spirit world which can make it a struggle to be in the harsh reality of the earth plane. You really just want to live in a perfect world where everything is peaceful and beautiful, so you can choose to ignore or overlook any harshness that is going on around you. You will naturally give more than you will receive, and this can be a hard life lesson. Your challenge is to ground yourself and to integrate your spiritual body into your human body so as to truly live and explore your life here in every way.

It is not uncommon for souls to have both their Sun and their Ascendant in the same sign of the zodiac. This happens when a soul chooses around dawn as their time of birth on the earth plane. Such people have a double dose of all the characteristics and traits that go with that star sign. I have also seen and interpreted astrology charts where the soul has all his planets and lessons in just two or three signs and two or three Houses. We are all different and we all choose different lessons to learn and paths to walk, and the intensity of these journeys. The stars we have chosen to guide us show how we can walk the path and what talents, gifts, and wisdom we can use to our benefit along the way.

# CHAPTER 10

# THE MOON SIGNS

*("Your sooky side and Mummy issues.")*

The Moon represents your emotional body and how you naturally feel and react on that level of understanding and awareness. Through understanding the Moon's placement in your Natal Chart, you can easily see how to work with your emotions and when to make the best use of the lunar energy. Your Moon sign also identifies your feminine side and how you view and feel about the divine feminine energy that exists within us all, whether we are male or female. We all speak different languages of love, and it is your Moon and your Venus placements that dictate what this language will be and how you will express it.

At this time of writing this in 2018, the energy of the Divine Feminine is on the rise so as we can all honour this powerful and essential part of ourselves. This beautiful, intuitive and compassionate side of us has been shut down and disempowered for far too long, and the earth plane and all who live here have suffered greatly for it. Balance is an essential part of nature and something we are all responsible for, however as we developed through the ages we have forgotten about the importance of balance and how fragile it can be. The indigenous people around the world know and understand the importance of this. But in the name of progress we, as a modern society, have and continue to put very little importance on this. It is this powerful inner Goddess energy that is rising up at this time, to find its long overdue place sitting alongside – equal in every way – to the divine masculine energy that also exists within us all.

The Moon is a powerful force that works closely with the element of water. Lunar energy controls the tides, and as the earth plane is around 70% covered in water, the Moon influences every ocean and every sea upon her. We, as human beings, are made up of around 60% water as well, and so the Moon, to some degree, can move and control us as well.

Your Moon placement also denotes the type of mother, or female figure that raises you, will be in this lifetime. Through understanding the attributes of the sign your Natal Moon sits in, you can better understand why you chose the mother you did, and what her main influences and teaching are for you. It's always important to remember here that sometimes are mothers, and fathers, teach us through being the embodiment of what we DON'T want to be or DON'T like. For example, a soul born with their Moon in Cancer may choose a mother who, rather than being incredibly compassionate, sensitive and understanding, is in fact the complete opposite. And so we learn through the negative experience of receiving no compassion to develop a deep compassion for ourselves and others.

For each of us, as individuals walking different soul journeys, the Moon's main purpose is to teach about our emotional make-up and how we can work with this energy to find peace and joy in our lives, rather than fight against the emotional tides. The following is a brief explanation of how the Moon operates and makes you "feel" within each sign of the zodiac.

## MOON IN ARIES

Souls born with their Natal Moon in Aries are strongly independent and spontaneous. When they want something – they want it NOW and so their temperament can become quite demanding and impatient when things do not happen in the timeframe they would like them to. Often souls with Arian Moons are not as self-confident as they appear to be. This lunar placement enables them to appear a lot stronger than they really are; they can push through emotional situations and move forward, but in doing so they tend to bury or not deal with the emotional pain or baggage involved. Those born with their Moon in Aries tend to have mothers who encourage them to be leaders and to be independent and have little time or energy for insecurities and childhood fears. By choosing to have their Moon in a Fire sign, these souls deliberately choose mothers who can teach them about the strength of independence and the use of their will.

## MOON IN TAURUS

If you are born with your Moon in Taurus then you are born wanting and needing security, comfort, and safety around you at all times. You tend to be attracted to the finer things in life and having such things around you makes you feel even more secure and comfortable in your life. As this is such a dependable lunar placement, souls born under this sign tend to marry or partner up with someone for life. They are much more interested in creating a steady and reliable home and family than they are in chasing around looking for their best option. Once the Moon in Taurus soul is hurt, however, forgiveness and letting go are extremely difficult and they can stubbornly hold on to hurts and grudges for as long as it takes for them to get over it. The mothers of those who have the Moon in Taurus tend to be very loving and affectionate. They instil in their children the importance of working hard, and having an appreciation for the money and material possessions that bring so much emotional comfort and security. When you choose to have your Moon in this Earth sign, you are also choosing a mother who will ground you and show you the value of stability and taking care of what you own.

## MOON IN GEMINI

With the Moon in Gemini, the soul is constantly evaluating, thinking and analysing all that they feel. They can spend so much time in their heads, conjuring up scenarios and the way things are going to play out, that they completely take themselves away from the facts and create their own truth – which can then become their own reality. It is important that these souls are taught to express honestly and openly all that they feel and to discuss such things so they can get to the root of their problems rather than just pretend that they have dealt with them, or that they don't exist. This lunar influence encourages lots of activity and busyness too, as well as fun and laughter. The soul with the Moon in Gemini doesn't really want to take life seriously, has an insatiable curiosity for anything new and different, and loves to entertain others and make them laugh. These souls have chosen mothers who will also be active people and will encourage independence in their children as they are often busy working mothers juggling many responsibilities. Being an Air sign, these mothers are often not as available for their children as they need to be; the learning of independence here is about having to cope for themselves at times as Mum is busy elsewhere.

## MOON IN CANCER

When you are born with the Moon in Cancer, you are extremely sensitive and usually very intuitive or psychic. It is quite common for you to feel and know things about others and about what is going on. With this placement, you are extremely empathetic and sympathetic, always attracting those who seek comfort and counselling when they need understanding and help. You are often what is known as an "emotional clearing house". This means that you, without knowing it, pick up the feelings and emotions of those you come in contact with; you absorb these from that person, allowing them to unconsciously release the negative energy that they are holding on to. If you have no idea where your Moon sits, yet frequently find yourself feeling sad, anxious, upset, angry or any other emotion after you have been in contact with other people, then the chances are your Moon is in Cancer. It is important for anyone with their Moon in Cancer, Pisces or Scorpio to make sure to ask for protection every day before facing the outside world, and also to ask that their emotional body be cleared of other people's negative energy at the end of every day. Having the Moon in Cancer is also a creative placement. This can be a wonderful way for the soul to release pain and joy in a constructive and therapeutic manner. These souls have chosen mothers who teach them about compassion and empathy for others; family-oriented mothers who can have a lot of fear for their children; mothers who may have to learn to "mother rather than smother" those that they love.

## MOON IN LEO

You can spot a child born with their Moon in Leo in any schoolyard around the world. They are the ones making the most noise and demanding the most attention. Leo energy has such a need to express itself, and when your emotions sit in this energy of expression they have no choice but to come out for all to see. It is no surprise that SO many famous actors, musicians, and other public figures have either their Sun or Moon in Leo. These souls carry a powerful charismatic energy and have a deep need to not only be noticed but to be admired and appreciated for all that they offer. Therefore, they can become hurt and unhappy when their best efforts are not rewarded or acknowledged by others. These souls love wholeheartedly and will give themselves 100% to love and to their partners. The soul with the Moon in Leo has chosen a mother who teaches them to use their own strength to be outgoing and fearless. She shows them how to best use their power so as they can get the kudos they need from life and reach the status/position they would like to achieve in the public eye.

## MOON IN VIRGO

If you are born with your Moon in Virgo you often have a great need to be in total control of life, and in particular to have control over your emotions. You not only have a great eye for detail, but also a great need to make sure that any job or project you are given is carried out bit by bit, detail by detail believing that in this way the only result will be "perfection". You need to have order and not chaos in your emotional life. Although you, like any of us, can get caught up in dramas, you tend to avoid such things and would rather fly under the radar than through it. When it comes to love, souls with the Moon in Virgo will put a lot of pressure on themselves to be the perfect partner and will also have the same perfection expectations of their partners. They can often have an idealised opinion of what a relationship is all about and don't see or understand how good they have got it. They can waste a lot of time striving for something better than what they already have. The soul who has chosen to have the Moon in Virgo will have a mother who is very organised, tidy and who, in their eyes, will always do everything the best and the most "perfectly". A boy with a Moon in Virgo can be very attached to his mother and look to choose a partner in life who can emulate her energy.

## MOON IN LIBRA

The sign of Libra rules relationships and so when the Moon sits in this sign of the zodiac, the soul is very at home and makes the balance and harmony of all relationships they are in a top priority. They will actively and purposefully work to create balance and harmony in every situation they come into, often feeling that this is their responsibility. The soul with the Moon in Libra is the most social of the Moon signs, loves to entertain as the host, as well as be involved in any social opportunity that is on offer. They are extremely gracious, and in their efforts to make everyone feel comfortable or at home, can appear almost shallow at times. Being the Air sign that they are, they like to keep things light and fun. This can be a very sensitive placement. Underneath what appears to be a non-stop effort to please and balance things out for everyone else, there lies an emotional soul whose real purpose is to find their own peace and balance; and can only see how to do so by pleasing and going along with others. The soul who is born with the Moon in Libra chose a mother who, to them, is beautiful. This mother will teach the soul a lot about the value of looking good and presenting yourself to the world attractively, as well as the importance of beauty in the world and what a powerful purpose it serves.

## MOON IN SCORPIO

Souls born with the Moon in Scorpio have possibly the most intensely sensitive placement of the zodiac. These souls feel everything that happens to them and around them deeply and make their decisions and choices through all that they feel. This can mean that everything is dictated by how they are feeling and this, of course, is not a rational or realistic way to operate. These souls can be extremely secretive and have a lot of fear of anyone knowing too much about them. However, they have a deep need for the truth and will not tolerate or trust anyone who lies to them or tries to keep the truth from them. Souls with the Moon in Scorpio have a great need for love and affection, but have so much fear that they will not be loved or even liked that they don't allow others to know too much about them in case that information is later used against them as ammunition. As children, they often believe that everyone can tell what they are thinking, and so give off energy of hiding something when in actual fact they are trying to protect their inner sensitivities. As a water sign, it is common for souls with the Moon in Scorpio to be highly intuitive and psychic. These souls chose mothers who teach them all about the emotional world and how to deal with what you feel, as well as provide spiritual education. They often see their mothers as women of extreme power and goodness, but who can sometimes be a bit scary too.

## MOON IN SAGITTARIUS

Just like the Sagittarian Sun sign, those born with a Sagittarian Moon sign have a great love for adventure, excitement, and fun. They are very social souls who love nothing more than to have a good time with friends or to go out and make new friends. The more the merrier, as far as these souls are concerned. To this end, although they are loyal, they are often more interested in what the next fun time is rather than when a friend might need them. Therefore, they are not always the best people to rely on. Much like a magpie chasing after anything that shines, they are constantly on the look for something brighter, shinier and more exciting. They tend to be adaptable people who can fit into any situation and get along with anyone. The worst thing you can do to a soul with their Moon in Sagittarius is try to control them or tie them down in any way. They will not tolerate having their wings clipped by anyone. If you are born with your Moon in Sagittarius you have chosen a mother who is extremely independent and very busy. The purpose of this mother is to teach the child self-reliance. The child of this mother will usually see her as the one person who knows and speaks their truth, and so will take everything their mother tells them as gospel.

## MOON IN CAPRICORN

Souls born with the Moon in Capricorn usually have had many, many lifetimes as warriors and those who took care of business. In these lifetimes they were responsible for the lives and welfare of others, and therefore there was little time or energy for emotions and feelings. For those born with this Moon sign, there will always be a feeling or attitude that makes them feel responsible for others and for things turning out the way that they are supposed to. These souls can be cautious when dealing with new things in their lives and struggle deeply with trusting the feelings of others, as well as their own deep emotions. As they have had so many lifetimes of dealing with reality and the facts, they are distrustful of emotions and the actions that strong feelings create. This is a very ambitious placement that gives the soul a great deal of focus and commitment to its own journey in life and the successes it can achieve. The mother of the soul with the Moon in Capricorn tends to be strict and has a lot of rules, especially regarding behaviour, which will be firmly enforced. She teaches her children that life is a serious business and only through hard work and discipline will they be able to achieve their dreams and success in life.

## MOON IN AQUARIUS

Souls born with the Moon in Aquarius tend to be much more comfortable with being "different" to everybody else, than those who are born with their Sun in Aquarius. They feel the need to be different and will pursue anything and everything that allows them to further this need. These souls can also, quite naturally and without realising it, play hard to get. In actual fact they are not playing; they just don't want to be caught. They are independent, so if you want to love and live with a soul with their Moon in Aquarius you must be prepared to give them plenty of freedom and space to be who they are, and to do what they want. They can be happy and comfortable in relationships where their partner lives in another town or country, or where their partner is a lot younger or older than they are. They do not need the security of a white picket fence in the suburbs and can quite happily live on the belief that home is where the heart is. These souls are revolutionary in their thinking and are well known for their inventions and their forward thinking. However, this can also make them feel quite isolated and alone, as finding someone else who really "gets" this side of them can be hard. The soul with the Moon in Aquarius chose a mother who dances to her own drumbeat. She is here to teach the soul to embrace who they are and all that feels natural to them, rather than to be a sheep like all the other sheep in the flock. To this end, she may be a little distant from her child as she walks her own path in her own way.

## MOON IN PISCES

From an esoteric perspective, souls born with the Moon in Pisces are what we call "touched by God". They have chosen, before they were born, to leave their mark on the world in some way – usually through some type of humanitarian work inspired by their connection to Spirit. They are here to bring spiritual energy to the earth plane through their work in some way and are highly sensitive and highly creative souls. Souls born with the Moon in Pisces are also very intuitive, and it is normal for them to see, hear and feel dead people; they are natural Mediums. This heightened sensitivity means that the work that they do has to come from the very heart of them – they channel their creativity and they are always attached to Spirit. (One of the most famous souls born with the Moon in Pisces was Michael Jackson, a man who wrote the most beautiful lyrics and who always talked of the love he felt for the people of the world, and in particular children.) They also often go through life, especially in childhood, with their heads in the clouds seeing the very best in everyone and everything around them. They can be so heartbroken when let down or when their dreams are shattered. Their beautiful and inspirational imaginations are really just their strong connection to the Spirit world, and they are always open to sharing their creations with those who appreciate such things. The soul with the Moon in Pisces chose a mother who is almost mystical. She has a very calming influence on the child and can be viewed by the child as being an Earth Angel. The soul chose this mother to teach them about holding that space of calm and lightness; this gives the soul the feeling of protection and guidance needed to do the work they chose to do for humanity.

# CHAPTER 11

# SATURN – BECOMING A GROWN-UP

*("Who's your Daddy?")*

The planets in the cosmos are constantly moving and as they do so they make their way through the 12 astrological Houses and through the 12 signs of the zodiac. Some planets, such as the Moon, the Sun, Mercury, Mars, Jupiter and Venus, move fairly quickly; these are known as the "inner planets" or the fine-tuning of our soul's journey. Others, such as Saturn, Uranus, Chiron, Neptune, and Pluto, move at a much slower pace and are known as the "outer planets". As their movements are slower, these planets tend to teach us lessons that are more challenging, more sustained and more intricate.

During our lifetimes on the earth plane, we are presented with different opportunities to learn our life lessons and to evolve our souls. Not only are there the usual everyday relationship, work and health issues, there are also major planetary events that occur during each lifetime that are likened to "next level" learning. These events happen to each of us at certain ages in our lives, and they are designed to enable us to remember our Contracts and to keep us on track.

We can call these events "initiations" as they initiate us into growth and invite us through the doors of change. They are vital life-changing experiences and the more awareness and significance we can give to them, the more use we can make of them to assist us to grow and become all that we have chosen to be.

The first of these major planetary events is known as your Saturn Return. From an esoteric astrology perspective, Saturn is the most important planet in the Natal or Birth Chart. He is the planet that identifies the greatest fears we have chosen to face in this lifetime, as well as where we will face the greatest challenges in this lifetime. He is our teacher and our disciplinarian. It takes Saturn approximately 2.5 – 3 years to work his way through a sign of the zodiac and approximately 28 – 30 years to work his way through all the 12 Houses (areas of learning) of your Birth Chart and return to the exact same spot where he was sitting at the time of your birth. The time period of his transit back to this spot is called your Saturn Return, with the first of these happening when you are 28 – 30 years old. Saturn will then carry on transiting your Natal Chart and you will experience your second Saturn Return at around the age of 58 – 60 years of age.

As Saturn is such a powerful teacher and ruler the significance of your Saturn Return is HUGE. From an astrological perspective, we do not believe that you are really an adult until you reach this time in your life. Saturn, being our teacher, needs all 28+ of those years to bring us lessons in every different area (House) of our lives and so until you have had a look and a try at all your life lessons, you are not considered to be an adult. To this end, something significant and life-changing will always occur for you between the ages of 28 and 30 to wake you up to the fact that you are now an adult and as such you must start taking responsibility for your own life on every level. Some souls may choose to get married at this age, or you may have your first child, or you may move to another town or country to live, or you may start a new career. Big things happen during this time period that challenge you to step up and take control of your life.

We are all affected constantly by the energy of the planets and the cosmos. As we approach our Saturn Return, we consciously and/or subconsciously feel this energy building; we may start to feel a lot more stressed, unsure and even helpless when we look at who and where we are, and what lies ahead of us. There is even a "group" or theory called the "27 – 29'ers Club" consisting of a lot of famous actors, singers and other public people, who have chosen to take their lives at around about this time, as the fear of the future and feelings of not being able to maintain public and private responsibilities becomes all too much. Your Saturn Return is a very real and powerful thing that you cannot avoid, but you can survive and most importantly you can gain the greatest learning from.

When I look at the planet Saturn I see him as a teacher. I liken him to that teacher you had at School whom you may not have liked very much as they demanded a lot from you, and probably told you off a whole lot too. When you look back at your school days however, this is the teacher you remember as they were the one who taught you the most and whom you gained the most respect for because of this. Saturn is a hard taskmaster, but he is actually not that hard to please if you play by his rules. His rules are: hard work, discipline, and focus. Just like back in School you know that when you worked hard, paid attention in class, and did your homework, you got the best marks and you achieved your best results. Never forget that as hard as the lessons of Saturn can be, he is also the planet who gives us the greatest rewards in life when we pass the tests.

Another important lesson from Saturn is around the choice of the father we wish to have in our lifetime, or the strong paternal influence we wish to have over us as children and throughout our lives. Saturn, being the teacher and disciplinarian, resonates with the energy of the father or the one who teaches and enforces the rules in your life. The sign you chose to have your Saturn sitting in, in this lifetime, will define the type of father you chose to have, and what he is here to teach you through your relationship with him. In some cases, if the mother or maternal figure is the dominant personality and influence in the family, rather than the father or paternal figure, then Saturn can represent her role in your life instead. From my experience, this is rare and only in cases where the mother is a very powerful energy within the home, consciously taking on the role of mother and father to the child. What is important to remember is that as souls choosing our parents we do not always choose them for their finer and more loving qualities. Sometimes we choose our parents so they can show us what NOT to do or be in life, rather than what we should aspire too.

Saturn moves through each sign of the zodiac at 2.5 – 3 year intervals. The learning he brings to each astrological sign is different yet requires the same degree of focus and attention. Not only is everything that he is trying to teach us what we need to learn on a personal level as part of our soul's journey through this lifetime, he is also teaching global lessons for the whole of planet earth to learn as a collective. The sign of the zodiac that your Saturn sits in at the time of your birth dictates how you will learn your greatest life lessons, and the House in your Chart that he is found in is the main arena where you will learn these lessons.

## SATURN IN ARIES

When you are born with Saturn in Aries you are born with life lessons to do with authority and how you can learn to rely upon and support yourself. Although you feel defiant, headstrong and self-centred, you do not like to assert your will and so you become frustrated with yourself and often end up bowing to the wishes of others simply because you didn't feel confident enough in yourself to say or do differently. You are here to learn to understand your strengths, to work with others and to be independent or to be a leader; you are a pioneer with a fear of leadership that you need to overcome. Learning to have more confidence in yourself and to have faith in your dreams can make you a great leader and/or pioneer in your field; but you must learn to deal with those whom you feel have authority over you with diplomacy and understanding, and stick up for yourself calmly yet firmly. The soul who chose to have Saturn in Aries has chosen a father who is authoritive, headstrong and who offers them rules and boundaries to work within. This father will teach them the value of leadership and putting your own needs first, however, this learning could come through the child feeling they have very little power to do things for themselves as Dad may always know best.

## SATURN IN TAURUS

Souls born with this placement have a strong purpose in life yet can become way too caught up in the material world, seeing this as the epitome of success in life. To this end, many souls with this placement struggle to get the balance right between working too hard and not working hard enough. For so long as the focus is on the bank balance and material gain, they find it hard to bend and compromise with those around them and the demands of their lives. The greatest life lessons here are to understand the value of inner peace and contentment over material gain and financial security. The soul born with Saturn in Taurus chose a father who will teach them about security and the material value of hard work. This father will usually expect their child to do chores so as they can understand how to create their own stability through work and perseverance. However, this father may not communicate well or be prepared to look at things from the child's point of view. Therefore, although the child may understand the need to work hard, they may not understand when and how to do so, and to this end can sway between that lazy way of being to a workaholic way of being.

## SATURN IN GEMINI

This placement is all about controlling the over-active mind and imagination. Gemini energy can be very scattered – all ideas and little action. Saturn in this sign is here to teach discipline through follow through, and how the best ideas are nothing without the necessary action to see them to fruition. Souls with this placement have life lessons in avoiding self-sabotage and in learning to apply ALL their energy to the result they wish to achieve, rather than just "winging" it, or hoping for the best. With your Saturn in Gemini you are also here to learn the value of accepting and expressing your insecurities and your shortcomings so as you can heal these and find a greater appreciation and respect for yourself. The soul who chose to have their Saturn in Gemini is choosing a father who can show them the variety and versatility of life. This father will be lots of fun, but not always available to the child as he may struggle to put as much time and effort into his family life as he does into his work life.

## SATURN IN CANCER

With Saturn in Cancer, the soul is constantly looking for validation and approval from others to allow them to feel truly worthwhile and necessary in this world. The soul is here to learn much about the importance of loving and nurturing themselves to feel strong and secure in life, rather than only being able to feel this way when someone else gives them the love they need. For so long as they seek this in the outside world they will struggle to be truly happy and at peace. Their life lesson is to love and value themselves over and above everyone else as this is the only truly sustainable way to survive. When a soul chooses to have Saturn in Cancer they are choosing a father figure who is to teach them about compassion and understanding for others. This can be taught through receiving the nurturing they need from him, or through the harsher lesson of not being nurtured but left to nurture themself. This father can help the soul to learn about the feelings and needs of others, but he can also encourage them to put more value on taking care of others than on taking care of themself.

## SATURN IN LEO

Souls with their natal Saturn in Leo tend to feel that they need to constantly prove to the world that they are its greatest gift. They live to impress, to take charge and find themselves extremely lost and confused when they are not given the attention and accolades that they believe they deserve for all that they do. Souls under this placement may often "buy" friends or pay for "publicity" that can show the world how fabulous they are. Their greatest life lesson is to learn that they have big and courageous hearts, and if they just allow this part of them to shine through they will undoubtedly always receive the kudos they so desire. The soul with Saturn in Leo is choosing a father who can teach them how to express themselves and how to be heard. This father could, however, put an unnecessary amount of emphasis on the importance of material possessions and professional success in life, along with all the kudos that such things can bring. The child can grow to believe that the admiration from others is more important than the friendship they have to offer.

## SATURN IN VIRGO

When you are born with Saturn in Virgo you tend to take life very seriously and deny yourself the pleasures of life. The Virgoan need for perfection is in charge, and the soul can struggle to see their own perfection, no matter how hard they work and how much attention they pay to detail. Their greatest life lesson is to understand that doing their best is who they are, and in believing in this they can live a happy AND successful life without unnecessary stress or self-made disappointment. With Saturn in Virgo, the soul chooses a father who will teach them the importance of doing a job or task to the best of their ability no matter what the circumstances. This father can be quite distant from his children at times, as he struggles to be everything to everyone. The challenge here is for the child to learn to understand perfection without feeling like they have to be perfect at all times.

## SATURN IN LIBRA

This placement is all about balance. Being born with this placement means that fairness and justice are extremely important to you, and you are here to learn about asserting yourself to create harmony, rather than feeling the need to step back and go along with everyone else to achieve this in your life. Saturn here encourages the soul to work with others for the highest good of all concerned. The greatest life lesson is to understand the importance of balance in every area of your life and to maintain this no matter what others may demand of you. The soul who chose to have Saturn in Libra chose a paternal figure in their life to teach them about balance. This father, however, could himself be someone who bends to the will of others more than he should, and the child grows up seeing and feeling that it is their responsibility to create that balance for others as well.

## SATURN IN SCORPIO

Scorpio energy LOVES power and so when task-master Saturn jumps in here this need for power is amplified and enforced. There is great resourcefulness with this placement as well as the ability to work hard to achieve goals – but at what cost? The major life lesson here is in the use of personal power. There is an element of ruthlessness with this placement, as well as the ability to truly see where others are coming from. This awareness can be as easily used negatively as it can positively. The soul is challenged to understand where it is appropriate to use their power over others, and where it is not. The soul who is born with Saturn in Scorpio chose a father who will teach them about the use of personal power and about how to use restraint and caution rather than leaping into things headfirst. This father will possibly be a powerful man in his own right; the soul may perceive him to be bigger and stronger in every way, and there may be some fear of upsetting or going against the will of this father figure.

## SATURN IN SAGITTARIUS

This placement encourages mastership of all that it touches. It does not wish to dabble in things – it wants to know it all, be it all and embrace the power and material gain that goes with this. Souls with this placement can want it all and want it all NOW. Their greatest lesson is to learn that through setbacks and challenges they can develop higher skills and real mastership of their talents. Developing patience and acceptance of their path at an early age will lead them to successful futures. The soul who chose to have Saturn in Sagittarius chose a father who can teach them about adventure, independence, and mastership. This father has been chosen so the soul can learn to step out of their shell and feel empowered to do so. However, this paternal figure could also be quite controlling and have high expectations for his children. To this end, the relationship could run hot and cold. As the young soul learns what freedom of choice feels like, they may rebel against the control and authority of this father figure.

## SATURN IN CAPRICORN

When Saturn sits in Capricorn, it is at home and therefore incredibly ambitious, focussed, determined and regimented, believing in a life of all work and little play. With this placement there is only one way forward; souls may initiate and face many battles to get what they want, the way they want it and when they want it. The greatest life lesson here is to learn to use compassion and empathy alongside your determination and ambition so as when you do arrive at your destination, you can truly enjoy it and all the rewards it brings. When the soul has their Natal Saturn in Capricorn, they chose a father who can be strict and very negative. This father will teach much to his children through the negative rather than the positive, which can result in a child growing up in fear or all the "what if's?" out there. This parent can always be relied upon for good solid advice, but that advice will always err on the side of caution. Depending on how much non-Capricorn energy they have in their Charts, the soul who has chosen this father figure will either resonate completely with their father's ways or run a mile from all those cautionary rules and regulations.

## SATURN IN AQUARIUS

Aquarian energy hates change, and so when Saturn sits in this sign he will bring home the lessons of accepting change and learning to embrace it through individuality and unique thinking. Souls with this placement can be successful in life so long as they are prepared to "face the fear and do it anyway". Their greatest life lesson is to find a way to be free yet still have order, stability and forward movement in their lives. Until they can learn to let go and let God, they will always trip over themselves and struggle to manifest their desires. The soul who has Saturn in Aquarius chose a father figure who may be quite detached or even simply not there much. This choice is all about independence and the ability to feel like you fit and that you are complete, no matter what anybody else says or thinks of you. This father could even be quite eccentric or a real rebel and is here to teach the soul to be themselves – no matter who that might be – and to acknowledge and enjoy all that is alternative out there.

## SATURN IN PISCES

Souls with this placement are here to learn a lot about self-discipline and facing up to the realities of life; therefore, life can teach them some harsh lessons. They are resourceful on the one hand but lack the ambition and resilience needed to put their highly creative and individualistic ideas into practise. Their greatest life lesson is to learn to face up to life, rather than running and hiding from it when the going gets tough. This can only come through learning to trust in their abilities, and in the world they live in. The soul who chose to have their Natal Saturn in Pisces chose a father who can teach them to be gentle, creative and to listen to their inner knowings and feelings. The father figure here may be quite quiet and unauthorative and so the maternal figure may have a lot more control and power in the home. Through this, the child is here to learn the balance of feelings and actions, when to run with these and when not too.

So, if for instance, you are born with Saturn in Pisces, at the time of your first Saturn Return you may well be faced with some big life lessons that will teach you to see how strong you truly are and how hard work and focus can really pay off for you when you stick to it.

When we are younger and faced with sudden changes in our lives that bring about fear and uncertainty, we will react in the way that we are the most comfortable or at home with. I will continue to use the scenario of the soul who reaches their first Saturn Return, at around 29 years of age, with Saturn in Pisces. They may have gotten to this age and worked for themselves in a few different jobs and careers and done reasonably well for themselves. However, they have never really challenged themselves to work particularly hard at anything, nor have they challenged themselves to do better and aim higher. Their Saturn Return hits and suddenly the job they had that was paying the bills, had lots of fun people associated with it and allowed them to be creative on occasion, is taken away from them. At the same time, their relationship ends so they now need to find somewhere else to live and heal a broken heart as well. The soul finds themselves unemployed and homeless, and completely lost, as there was no back-up plan. Suddenly the big wide world out there is unfriendly and the enemy. Saturn Return is reminding them that they have many gifts and talents, and that they owe it to themselves to be the best they can be at what they do, and that they have a hidden stash of resilience that they have never had to call on until now. However, they lack ambition, and they are so sensitive to rejection that they are paralysed with fear as to what on earth they can do next to change this. It feels like their world is falling apart. However, their Higher Self and other Spiritual Guides and Helpers are standing by, offering synchronicities in the form of opportunities, new people, new places and chance encounters that offer a way not only through this challenging time, but through to amazing success on the other side. They just need to be brave enough to take that step out of the not-so-comfortable-any-more comfort zone and face the world in all its glory. If they choose at this pivotal astrological time, when the rewards are there as opportunely as the challenges are, to stay in fear, feeling very hard done by and sorry for themselves, then things will either go from bad to worse, or they will stay much the same with nothing, on the limited horizon to strive towards or aim for. On the other hand, if they can see the loss of their job and their partner leaving as an opportunity for growth and change, seize the advantages that come their way and/or capitalise on the chance encounters, then they will be rewarded with a new path. This path allows them to increase their creative skills and talents, to meet new and interesting people, and to embrace a new and successful chapter of their life.

The earth plane provides us with an arena to learn in, and the planets bring the lessons to this arena for us to master. Another factor, that is by far the most important one, is the role YOU allow yourself to play in all of this.

Your life is pre-destined in the sense that you are here to learn certain things, develop certain skills, meet certain people, live in certain places, have certain experiences, etc, etc. HOW you do all of this is the key to it all. Your 'free will" is only as powerful and as life-changing as you allow your perspective on your life to be. For so long as you feel like you are a victim of circumstances, or that everyone else has a better life than you, or that everything that happens to you is never your fault, you are a complete and utter victim. You have stripped yourself of your power, denied your intuitive nature and completely ignored the signs and communications that your Guides and Spiritual Helpers are bringing to you.

*YOU are the master of your destiny and YOU really do hold all the power – you just need to remember how to use it*

Your Saturn Return is your wake-up call to start not only participating more readily and actively in your soul's journey but to face what you fear the most. When you face your fears, they melt away into insignificance and they stop having power over you.

# CHAPTER 12

# URANUS OPPOSITION – MID-LIFE CRISIS TIME

*("Hold onto your broomstick. It's a wild ride ahead.")*

The next major planetary movement or initiation that occurs to affect us all on our personal soul journeys, is the Uranus Opposition or as we astrologers like to call it the "mid-life crisis"!!

This happens to everyone between the ages of 38 and 42, so at around about 40 years of age. From a planetary perspective, this means that Uranus, the planet of sudden and unexpected change (Mr. Curve Ball), has moved through half of the signs of the zodiac and is now sitting in exactly the opposite sign, House and position to the one he was at the time of your birth. He is opposing himself, and as we all know opposition more often than not relates to change, upheaval and friction.

The purpose of this planetary movement is to teach us about change, and about the importance of putting our own soul journeys and ourselves first in life. Change really is the only constant in life, and yet most of us do not like it one little bit and tend to resist it and fight against it when it is presented to us. When change is thrown at you, especially if you weren't expecting it or planning for it, it has the ability to throw your life and the way you are living it into disarray. So, if you look at the age of 40 as being when you are approximately half-way through your incarnation on the earth plane, you can see that the Uranus Opposition is all about giving your life a good shake up so as you can look at it through different eyes and from a different perspective, and work with any changes that are needed here. However, because the humanness of us does not like change and likes to think everything that goes wrong has got to be someone else's fault, the immediate reaction is to pass the blame. The one we blame is often the one we are the closest to thus it is no surprise that most divorces and separations happen at around about the age of 40.

What is really happening is that you are getting a chance to decide whether you wish to carry on being the person you are now (doing the same job, perhaps married to the same person, living in the same place and doing the same thing every day) or are you going to change this? You are being given the opportunity to take a good hard look at the life you are living and to decide what you would like to carry on with, what you would like to leave behind, and what you would like to change.

For most women, this time of life is often about coming into their own personal power. Perhaps you have spent the first 40 years of your life being the mother, taking care of your children, and making sure that your home is meeting everyone's needs in every way. In doing all of this you found that you had been too busy to embrace your own career and to follow your dream of becoming, let's say, a Music Teacher. You have, over these years, encouraged your children to learn music, perhaps you even taught them and perhaps now and then you allow yourself to get lost in this beautiful gift that you brought to the world. But your childhood dreams of learning and teaching music have never been fulfilled. The awareness of this has been creeping up on you for years, as we all subconsciously feel the movement of the planets as a reminder of our Contracts and soul journeys. With this awareness, perhaps resentment has also built up. You didn't get to do what you wanted to do; yet your husband did. You supported him to reach his goals and fulfil his dreams, yet yours were left by the way-side perhaps underneath a pile of laundry and dirty dishes. Once Uranus moves into opposition with his Natal self, all of these feelings and resentments not only raise their ugly heads to be acknowledged, but they start to weigh heavy on you. The humanness of you will more often than not turn to the husband/partner and put the blame on them. Your Ego Self is now stepping into its full glory and it wants revenge for all that it feels you have been "forced" to put to one side for the sake of another. In actual truth, it is not your partner, your children or anyone else's fault that you are not where you would like to be, doing what you would like to do and living the way that you always thought you would. It's quite simply YOUR fault, and now, with the support of your Uranus Opposition, you get the chance to change it.

What you, as a woman, are being encouraged to do at this time is speak up, exercise your personal power, ignite the Higher Self part of you, and start to make and be the changes you wish to see in your life. It is no-one's fault but your own that you are not already doing this, except for one other very important aspect - TIMING. So, at 40, what better time to start a new journey or take another path? You are still young, your children probably don't need your undivided attention any more, and you have the gifts and talents you brought with you waiting to be used, and your Contract and soul journey to adhere too.

At around 40 years of age you have the support of the cosmos to make significant changes in your life. You may choose to go down the path of divorce and have your life turned upside down by all that this represents, or you may choose to go back to school to learn to be that Music Teacher, or perhaps you already have the qualifications and you can now actually become that Music Teacher. The important thing is that you do choose to change, and you choose to do so for your own highest good and to honour who you truly are.

For men the Uranus opposition/mid-life crisis is slightly different. For men it is very much about the awareness of their own mortality and virility. They discover that their power, that "manly" power they have had in their lives over women, over other men and within their careers, is perhaps diminishing; they no longer feel like they have the ability to attract what they desire. They are looking forward and seeing a life where everything seems ho-hum...same old job, same old wife, same old car etc, etc. And so, they look to what they can add to their lives to feel that thrill again. Men, at the end of the day, are hunters and seekers, and so this drive within them needs to have an outlet of some kind, or they lose their zest for life. This is where we can see why men of this age have affairs, buy expensive sports cars, or distance themselves from their daily reality in some way. They too are feeling that push of change, and they have their own primal and instinctual way of dealing with these feelings. (I would like to point out here that I am not saying that it is only men who behave in this way, and only women who behave as in the other example I gave. The roles can easily be reversed, and of course, both parties can play the same game too.)

*Your Uranus Opposition/mid-life crisis is one of the most powerful periods in your entire lifetime to make the necessary changes you need to. This opportunity is given to you so you can live the second half of your life in fulfilment of all you wish it to be, and you have the support of the cosmos behind you every step of the way.*

I will now introduce you to the Uranus Opposition/mid-life crisis polarities that can occur, depending on the placement of the planet Uranus in your Natal Chart.

## NATAL URANUS IN ARIES – URANUS OPPOSITION IN LIBRA

When you are born with Uranus in Aries in your Natal Chart you are quick thinking, reactive and often a pioneer of new more unconventional ways of doing and being. You tend to be focussed on yourself and have a great need to do things your way. When you reach your Uranus Opposition you are being awoken to the need to look at the whole of humanity's needs, or your community's needs, and to find the right balance between putting yourself first and doing what is best for the higher good of all concerned. Your mid-life crisis could very much be about you having to learn to accommodate and empathise more with others rather than being only focussed on your life and your way of thinking and being.

## NATAL URANUS IN TAURUS – URANUS OPPOSITION IN SCORPIO

The soul born with Uranus in Taurus is incredibly determined, stubborn and methodical in all that they do. They could have many fears regarding money and security in their lives and to this end can be materialistic and overly focused on what they can earn and own in their lives. They tend to operate within the arena of only what they can see and know right in front of them being relative, and struggle to see life from any other point of view but their own. The mid-life crisis experience for these souls can bring all of their fears and insecurities to the surface. The purpose of this is to allow them to see that money is not the answer, and that they can achieve security and peace in life through what they know and feel, rather than through what they own.

## NATAL URANUS IN GEMINI – URANUS OPPOSITION IN SAGITTARIUS

Souls born with Uranus in Gemini are quick thinking, busy and the ultimate multi-taskers. They are full of ideas, inventions and imagination but for all of this busyness in their heads they can struggle to put their dreams into action and constantly find themselves right back at the start again with very little gain. During their mid-life crisis the native Uranus in Gemini souls have the opportunity to learn to master their skill(s) and to use their powerful imaginations to move forward and take control of their lives and their destinies.

## NATAL URANUS IN CANCER – URANUS OPPOSITION IN CAPRICORN

When Uranus sits in Cancerian energy in the Natal Chart, the soul is very sensitive to others and usually highly intuitive and psychic. They may go through life finding that words and messages just pop out of their mouths to guide others. They are natural Channels for spiritual communication. Due to the unpredictability of Uranus in the overly-sensitive sign of Cancer, they can come across as being quite eccentric and "out there" and to this end can enjoy more non-traditional relationships with others. The mid-life crisis here gives them the ability to ground themselves and use their sensitivity and psychic awareness for a purpose that can help and assist other souls along their journey.

## NATAL URANUS IN LEO – URANUS OPPOSITION IN AQUARIUS

Uranus in Leo is full of bravado, courage and determination to be not only heard and noticed, but to be the leader and to rule the roost. This placement wants to take over and be the action that is necessary for change, however it can be rash and foolhardy as its quest for fame and fortune can take over from what is worthwhile and practical. This mid-life crisis is all about the soul looking to where it can lead for the higher good of all concerned, and when used correctly can bring great compassion, understanding and humanitarian awareness to their leadership abilities.

## NATAL URANUS IN VIRGO – URANUS OPPOSITION IN PISCES

When the soul is born with Uranus in Virgo, they have a great need for order amongst the chaos. They really struggle with those who are not organised, or who don't care to work with systems and methods that are about making life easier and that can help to make a difference in the long term. They can be quite rigid in their daily lives, and tend to need concrete proof of things rather than just being able to accept and/or "feel" what is best for them. During their mid-life crisis they may find themselves dealing with the collapse of structures around them that have outgrown their use. They will instead be asked to rely on faith and to create a belief system that they can feel supported by.

## NATAL URANUS IN LIBRA – URANUS OPPOSITION IN ARIES

The soul with Uranus in Libra is concerned with the welfare of others, keeping the peace and finding balance in their lives. Yet there can also be a rebellious quality to these souls. They can attract and create sudden and unexpected events into their lives designed to test their need for harmony; this can make decision-making challenging for them. The mid-life crisis experiences for these souls are all about learning to have faith in their choices and decisions and not being afraid to stand up and take charge of their own lives, and the lives of others if need be.

## NATAL URANUS IN SCORPIO – URANUS OPPOSITION IN TAURUS

When the soul is born with Uranus in Scorpio they are here to learn about their own personal power and their sexual energy, and how to use both of these for the higher good of all concerned.

Their ability to look deeply into things can result in them seeing themselves from different perspectives, and this can cause illusions and disillusions about who they truly are. In their mid-life crisis they have the opportunity to learn to have more control, structure and security in their lives. This will ensure a solid base beneath them, no matter what curve ball is thrown their way, so as they can work with the reality of their strengths and weaknesses rather than just being focussed on the need for power.

## NATAL URANUS IN SAGITTARIUS – URANUS OPPOSITION IN GEMINI

Souls born with this placement are here to master all that they do and to do so for their own advancement as well as the evolution of the planet as a whole. They easily get caught up in their way being the only way; the downside to this is total preoccupation with a certain belief, religion, rule or theory. Their mid-life crisis enables them to calm down and use the power of communication to not only talk more about what they believe, but to learn to listen to what others have to say as well, so as they can find an acceptable use for their knowledge and power.

## NATAL URANUS IN CAPRICORN – URANUS OPPOSITION IN CANCER

Capricorn energy is all about structure and concrete foundations. This placement will encourage people to be constructive in their lives and easily break from any old ways that are not sustainable so that new formats that will last the distance can be introduced into their lives. This energy can be quite cold and calculating, very much concerned with what it is best for the person involved rather than for humanity as a whole. During their mid-life crisis they will learn about motivation and action from a more compassionate and nurturing perspective; in other words, learning to do what is best for themselves and for others with love and understanding.

## NATAL URANUS IN AQUARIUS – URANUS OPPOSITION IN LEO

Uranus is at home in Aquarius. Fully activated it brings out one's most inventive, unique, technological and forward-thinking sides, an excellent energy for inventors and creative souls who think and operate outside the box. The energy for being "different" can be strong, and makes these souls feel at times like they are not understood or accepted for who they truly are. This is a very powerful mid-life crisis where the soul can learn to not only love and embrace themselves on every level, but take all their "quirkiness" out there to the world as leaders and extroverts.

## NATAL URANUS IN PISCES – URANUS OPPOSITION IN VIRGO

When Uranus sits in Pisces it is considered to be extremely creative and expressive. This is the energy of actors and those who are not afraid to let their inner creativity shine. However, these souls can be so busy "finding" themselves and uncovering their talents that they neglect to participate in the real world. Their mid-life crisis is all about taking all that creativity and finding a concrete and practical use and/or outlet for it, so that they can find success in life and share it with the world.

# CHAPTER 13

# CHIRON – THE WOUNDED HEALER

*("When a bandage is just not enough.")*

Chiron is known as the "wounded healer". This is a small planet that was discovered in the 1970's. Unfortunately, not all astrologers recognise Chiron as a planet or the healing force that it is. Within esoteric astrology, it is considered to be an extremely important part of your astrological make-up as it defines the wounds that you brought with you into this lifetime to heal. Once you have done the necessary healing work, Chiron's placement in your Chart then goes on to show you how and where you can teach and heal others through your knowledge and experiences. Chiron has an unusual orbit which runs between Saturn and Uranus, making Chiron the Rainbow Bridge between reality and imagination, or between what is and what could be.

The most important thing about Chiron from the esoteric astrology perspective is that he rules Virgo. Traditional astrology puts Mercury as the ruler of Virgo, but we beg to differ here. Virgo souls arrive on the earth plane with a great need to heal both themselves and others, and so they have this natural understanding of the pain that we carry and the weight of this to our souls. Therefore, it makes perfect sense, that the sign that is here to heal and be healed should be ruled by the planet that is responsible for such things.

The placement of Chiron in your Chart shows where you will most need emotional healing so as you can become stronger and more learned through your experiences here. The placement shows where you may lack confidence, which creates the wound of worthiness. The wounds of Chiron are ones which mean that due to how we feel about ourselves, we distance ourselves from others, do not reach out when help is there, or just judge ourselves so harshly that we don't even want to acknowledge that we have any value whatsoever. Chiron shows us the way to heal ourselves from self-imposed wounds. Once we have mastered these, he gives us the power to hand this same knowledge and healing on to others – but the lesson of Chiron is that YOU must do the work first.

This is a similar lesson with all the planets and their effect on us as souls having the human experience. As above so below, so we take what the planets give to us and we make it work for us down here. There are similar lessons here that are brought to us through what others mirror back to us. Part of the early learning of Chiron will mean that we will attract to us those who also have the same hurts and wounds. Through seeing how they react and how they experience these, we can gain a more objective look at ourselves, and see what we need to change and heal within ourselves.

It takes this powerful little planet 50 – 52 years to do its circuit around the Sun and through all the Houses in your Natal Chart, and so your first (and for most of us only) Chiron Return comes at this stage of your life. By the time you are around 50 years of age, you have had plenty of experience in the game of life. You have lived, loved, worked, laughed, cried and so much more, but have you dealt with your greatest wound and are you healed? If, by the time you reach around 50 years of age, you have learned the lessons of Chiron and healed that deep wound within yourself, then congratulations to you and you will be rewarded by the energy of the astrological sign that your Chiron has now returned to. I would encourage anybody reading this book and on their spiritual journey to look to where you feel the most insecure, where you can be hurt the most, and/or where you have been through the most painful experiences of your lifetime to date, and begin the healing process. The healing power and rewards of Chiron are as significant in your life as the rewards of learning the lessons of Saturn. Saturn deals with your fears, Chiron with your wounds, and these powerful initiations can be closely linked to one another. Both of these planets teach us that when we heal ourselves, face our fears and believe in who we truly are, then we connect ourselves to the oneness that we all a part of. We start to feel the power of togetherness and the unconditional love that this holds for us all.

## CHIRON IN ARIES

The soul born with Natal Chiron in Aries brings with them the pain of not being good enough. Often souls who have chosen this placement have let others down in another lifetime, and they are here this time around bearing that pain, and looking to heal themselves by becoming the leaders, those who can be trusted and relied upon. Souls with this placement can feel quite nervous and insecure; they compensate for this by being competitive, determined to be noticed, to be of use and to be believed in. The more the Soul with Chiron in Aries can learn to be independent of others and comfortable in their own skin, the faster they will heal, and the more quickly they will be able to heal and teach others. They are here to be pioneers of new ways, to lead others forward towards what needs to be done, and to do this openly and with wholehearted belief in themselves and all they have to offer.

## CHIRON IN TAURUS

When you are born with your Chiron sitting in Taurus, you are born with a great fear of not being safe, secure and comfortable in life. Perhaps you are coming from a lifetime where you lost everything, or from a lifetime where you put no value on what you had. Your answer to healing this wound in this lifetime may be to choose to surround yourself with lots of beautiful possessions to fill that need for security, but really this only puts a bandage over the wound. You are here to learn how to feel safe and secure from within and to understand that no amount of money or material comfort can heal this. Your safety and security in life comes from loving and believing in yourself, and not from what you can buy, accumulate and hide behind. You are steady, methodical and steadfast in all that you do, and this is your healing gift to the world. The more you can open yourself up to life and all that it brings, the less insecure you will feel. The more you allow yourself to communicate what you are feeling and ask for help when you need it, the more you will realise that you are not alone and that you are always loved and taken care of.

## CHIRON IN GEMINI

Souls born with Chiron in Gemini are bringing with them the pain of not being understood. Your greatest asset is your ability to communicate, but this is also your greatest detriment. Learning to think before you speak, and to allow your truth to be the real truth and not just the truth you wish to hear or that you wish others to hear is your greatest challenge. Your wounds of being misunderstood and not appreciated for your words in other lifetimes weigh heavily on you. You feel you should perhaps bend, manipulate and change the truth so as it will be more acceptable to yourself and to others. You can also use gossip to hide behind, rather than allowing open and constructive conversations to be your vehicle. For so long as you keep embellishing the facts, or talking too much about inconsequential things, you are running from your pain. Your challenge is to allow the truth to be heard, no matter what it might result in; the truth may hurt, but it will also set you free.

## CHIRON IN CANCER

If you are born with your Natal Chiron sitting in Cancer, you are born with a lack of self-love and a deep fear that you are not loved or cared for by anyone. This can cause you to behave in one or two ways. You either distance yourself from everyone in the belief that they will hurt you as badly as you fear they will. Or, you try to make yourself as indispensable and necessary in the lives of others as you can, so that you can be worthy of their love. As long as you feel so worthless, you put this huge protective shell around you that others cannot penetrate, and all you want is for them to break through it. Your challenge is to learn to love yourself more than anyone else can love you. In doing so you learn the true value of nurturing and compassion. Your ability to feel deeply gives you the ability to empathise with others. Once you have learned the lesson of self-love, you naturally encourage others to see what they can love about themselves and gently and compassionately heal and teach them how worthwhile and necessary they are.

## CHIRON IN LEO

The soul born with Chiron in Leo is here to understand and heal the pain of not being everything to everyone. In another lifetime you perhaps had the world at your feet and then it all turned sour on you. You come into this lifetime feeling like you have to be noticed, have to admired, and have to stand out in some way. Your greatest fear is often being made fun of or being ignored, and a deep anger and resentment can build within when you are treated this way. Your challenge is to become everything you need to be to yourself. It does not matter what another soul thinks of you, or how much they respect and admire you, if you cannot feel the same way about yourself. You have nothing to prove and no-one to prove it too. Once you have healed this deep wound within yourself, you then have the ability to heal others through encouragement, positivity and being an inspiration to them on every level.

## CHIRON IN VIRGO

The soul born with Chiron in Virgo has the deep wound of uselessness. They are born doubting that anything they do is good enough; no matter how hard they try, they can never be as good as, talented as, or beautiful as, the person standing next to them. They have a huge fear of being criticised and even the slightest comment, constructively directed at them, can feel like a tidal wave of judgement coming their way. This is a very sensitive placement, one that identifies perhaps more than one lifetime of being victimised and punished for not achieving or not reaching someone else's standards. These souls can heal themselves by listening and absorbing all that others say to them, without judging it or looking for the negatives. This soul can run themselves into the ground trying to live up to expectations that are only in their own heads – no-one else's. Their challenge is to learn to not sweat the small stuff, to allow themselves to just "let go and let God" rather than feel that they must hold on to the steering wheel of life in case they crash and fail. The ability to work with the details in life means that the healing and teaching they can offer will never leave a stone unturned in getting down to what needs to be dealt with. They can set up systems and structures that support all that they do; by doing so they can let go of fears of not being good enough, as there is now a firm basis to create and expand from.

## CHIRON IN LIBRA

If you chose to be born with your Chiron in Libra, you chose to understand the importance of deep balance. Souls with this placement have often had past lives where they were abandoned and rejected by others and come into this lifetime with a great fear of being alone. To this end, they can not tolerate being on their own in any way and so will go out of their way to fit in with others or go with the flow, as to them anything is better than being alone. True balance comes from being at peace with yourself and not feeling that you are responsible for the harmony of others. These souls' greatest healing comes from realising that they are not here to please everyone else, only themselves. They don't need to put up with being treated badly just so they don't have to be on their own. The soul with their Chiron in Libra tends to be able to see how others can find balance and happiness in their lives, but they struggle to do this for themselves as the belief that the happiness of others determines their own personal happiness is so very strong. Once they have achieved their own balance between giving and receiving in life, they can heal and teach others through their wise and experienced counselling.

## CHIRON IN SCORPIO

Souls born with Natal Chiron in Scorpio are deeply sensitive and here to learn from emotional pain. They have brought with them into this lifetime a deep belief that if there is no pain, then there is no gain. They allow themselves to accept pain and hurt as part of life, and the more they submerge themselves in this belief the more powerless and emotionally damaged they feel. They are aware however, that allowing others to see their pain or know what hurts them is a dangerous thing, and so they hide their hurt behind bravado and laughter, pretending they are not hurt even when their hearts are breaking. Once it is healed and understood, this deep feeling is transformational for the soul as it shows them the depths they can descend to and ascend from as well. As they are so aware of what it feels like to be hurt and to be the victim of bad behaviour, they can offer deep emotional healing to others, but only once they have learned how to heal themselves. When they can move out of victim mode and learn what all they are feeling is teaching them, they make formidable teachers for others in pain, as they have infinite patience and unlimited understanding of how everything in life can make you feel.

## CHIRON IN SAGITTARIUS

If you are born with Chiron in Sagittarius, you are born fearing that you don't know enough. Souls with this placement often come from lifetimes of being spiritual or religious leaders, and they have mis-used this power resulting in them being condemned and judged for their actions. The soul with Chiron in Sagittarius has a great fear of freedom and of what would happen and what they would do if there was no control or no structure to life. Therefore, they try to control and manage every aspect of their lives, in the hope that in doing so all bases will be covered and therefore everything will turn out well. They can constantly argue about anything, as when someone disagrees with them or has a different interpretation of events, they see it as a threat to their knowledge and their know-how. The person with Chiron in Sagittarius is here to learn to expand and develop themselves freely without fetters, restrictions and control, and to also allow others the same degree of freedom and liberty. These souls, once they have learned their lessons, have a great ability to encourage others to also let go of what restricts them and stops them from being free and open in every way.

## CHIRON IN CAPRICORN

Chiron in Capricorn souls are here to learn about trust, and deeply trusting in themselves and in the process of life. These souls often see hard work and discipline as the only way forward in life, and so they can strip their lives of any joy or fun as such things are considered to be a waste of valuable time. They can become so obsessed in being someone and getting somewhere that they forget to actually live, love and enjoy their lives and all that the earth plane has to offer. They often come from lifetimes where they have been victimised and made to feel like they are incompetent and incapable of amounting to anything. In this lifetime they are on a mission to prove everyone wrong. These souls are here to learn to be present in the moment and to enjoy every minute of life for what it brings – both good and bad. Once they learn to trust in themselves and in the process of life, they can find joy and fun in so much more and they then learn about life's rewards. Their healing gift to others is to teach them to be diligent, while having faith and trust in the process so they can replace their negative outlook on life with a more positive and joyful one.

## CHIRON IN AQUARIUS

If you are born with Chiron in Aquarius, you are born feeling that you don't fit in and you can therefore be completely disillusioned with life on the earth plane. It's as if you had such high hopes for life, and then it happened…! You feel intensely the lack of humanity in the world, and you wish to heal this over and above healing yourself. You have a huge hurt where in another lifetime you did not do enough to help those who could not help themselves, or you were responsible for badly treating humanity in some way, and so you are back to understand and heal the other side of this. You can go through life constantly feeling like it is a let down and not what you signed up for. Your healing comes through accepting that this is what you chose, so why not participate in it, and make the very best of it, rather than running from it. This can result in a very cynical outlook on life at times, that you are here to learn to give no energy too. The sooner the soul with their Chiron in Aquarius can learn to accept all that life throws at them, and to participate in life rather than feeling safer just observing it from the side-lines, the more alive and happy they will feel. Their gift of healing to others comes from encouraging others to do what they can to help one another, and to look for the beauty and strength in humanity and in themselves, rather than focussing on what makes us feel weak and inconsequential.

# CHIRON IN PISCES

The soul born with Chiron in Pisces is very sensitive and often would like nothing more than to disappear into their own secret world of fantasy and imagination. This inability to cope with the harshness of the earth plane can make these souls shy and unwilling to stand up for themselves or to follow their dreams. They often come from lifetimes of being in service to Spirit but where they were persecuted for this, and so they prefer to remain in the background to escape notice. The soul with Chiron in Pisces has a very strong connection to Spirit. As Chiron is considered to be the Rainbow Bridge between the earth plane and the Spirit world, these souls can be natural channels for spiritual wisdom and teaching. They bring great wisdom with them into this lifetime, but they often feel worthless and are easily overwhelmed by too much pressure or responsibility. Their challenge is to push through the sensitivity they feel so they can share openly and unconditionally all that they know, feel and see. Once they have learned to put a worth on all that they are and all that they have to offer, they can heal and teach others the same empathetically and with great patience.

# CHAPTER 14

# THE MANY LAYERS OF LEARNING

*("Smashing your own glass ceiling")*

How do we go about changing our perspective and finding a way to learn our lessons without needless suffering? The answer is detachment and being kind to ourselves – self-love and self-awareness.

Let's say you have chosen in this lifetime to learn lessons in self-love and self-worth. As part of your plan to learn this, you invited (before you were born) other souls to come into your life to teach you this. The first person you chose in this scenario was your mother. You chose her with the full knowledge that she could help your soul to evolve, and once again remember that you made that choice whilst fully in your Higher Self energy. Her role is to help you to learn to love yourself first and foremost. Although she does love you very much, throughout your childhood she put you down, told you that you weren't clever enough or attractive enough to go anywhere in life, etc. due to her upbringing, skills and perspective on life. Perhaps she believed that by telling you this you would not be let down later in life and you would have a more "realistic" outlook on life. But whatever her "human" reasons for this were, her soul and your soul know that what she was really trying to teach you was to love yourself. For most of us, nothing teaches us more permanent and sustainable lessons in life than having to stick up for ourselves and put ourselves first. And more often than not, it is by being put down and made to feel that we are not good enough that we start to learn our own worth.

So, you have this mother who has cared for your needs and been your mother, but your soul needed more than that – it needed to be nurtured, loved and cherished for all that it was. As you grow and spend more time in the big wide world, you start to see that perhaps you can be someone and do something fantastic in this life – no matter what your mother said to you. You start to experiment with your own perspective; you develop more confidence in yourself through the support of friends and by embracing some of your gifts and talents. Yet the wound is still there. You have perhaps started to heal the outside edges of it, but it is still festering for the most part. You then attract to you a partner whose role (on that soul level) is also to teach you about your worth and value in life. That partner has their own perspective on who you are and where you need to be in their life, and perhaps has lessons to learn in control, anger, and jealousy for instance. All you wanted was someone to love you, as deep within you felt that no one could or would. Suddenly there is someone who can be all that the "wounded you" needs. But as you are wounded, the energy you are giving out will just attract similar energy back; and so you attract to you a partner who is also wounded. The relationship with this person, whom you feel you love and who you believe loves you, becomes abusive to you. Being with this person, whom you have given your love and trust to in the belief that they will "complete" and heal you, becomes a place where you are manipulated and abused. All the self-love and self-worth that you were precariously holding on to, is destroyed once again. During this, however, there is ALWAYS a little voice inside of you saying, "it doesn't have to be like this" and/or "you deserve better than this". One day, your Guides and Angels bring you an experience that allows you to see beyond what is happening to you, so as you can understand what you are being forced to learn. Perhaps a friend, whom you love very much, dies (as part of her contract with you to help you learn and as part of her own soul's journey as well). Through this heart-breaking experience, you can change your perspective. You realise that your life is worth more than misery and abuse every day; it is a gift to be lived and enjoyed as it can be taken from you at any moment. Suddenly, you start to get your power back; you start to see that you do have a worth. You start actually accepting and absorbing all those compliments about the way you look and/or the work that you do. You start to see your own beauty and your own value. And in finding this, you also find the strength to ditch the abusive partner and honour yourself in all your glory. You are healing that festering wound. As you get older and see things from an adult perspective, you begin to understand how you fit in, and how your life's ups and downs are presented to you as opportunities to grow and to evolve. Still, though there is work to be done as for every step we take, there is always a test or two along the way.

The next challenge is the new job. You are hired in a great role and you are so pleased with yourself; then a colleague whom you respect and admire starts to put you down and challenge you. With your newfound awareness of learning and a stronger, healthier belief in yourself, you now know that you have a choice in how you are going to react to this treatment. Your self-love has been activated and that little voice inside of you is not so little anymore. In fact, it's shouting at you. "You are amazing, and you don't have to accept this other person's opinion of you as being true".

Your Higher Self is guiding you and reassuring you of your soul purpose – to learn self-love – and you also now have the maturity and the perspective to see this treatment for what it is. The younger, less evolved you would have cried, run to the boss to complain, felt devastated and/or lost all confidence. But this new you, quite simply, understands that the other person's opinion of you is just that - their opinion - and it has no power over you unless you allow it too.

One of my most trusted methods to understand life lessons is the analogy of the onion with all its layers. Each of the scenarios mentioned in this chapter is a layer of the onion being peeled back in order to reach the core – the true YOU. We slowly but surely peel back a layer to expose what is underneath, and we keep peeling back and exposing our wounds until we get down to the core hurt, and right underneath that lies the true and real YOU.

*YOU are the master of your own destiny*
*YOU are the one with all the power*
*YOU are the one who decides what is good for you and what is not*
*YOU are a gift to the world – and no one may tell you differently*

# CHAPTER 15

# YOUR SPIRITUAL HELPERS AND PAST LIVES

## *("Working with them upstairs")*

At any given time, we are each surrounded by around 20 Spiritual Helpers, Angels, Guides, Masters, or loved ones who have passed over. It is the job of these enlightened beings to nudge us and guide us along our life paths according to the journey we have chosen (Natal Chart). In the scenarios that I gave to you in the previous chapter, the soul, who was grappling with these deep emotional issues, became aware of this guidance and support and allowed herself to act upon it rather than turn away from it. Once again this was a consciously done but it was inspired by their Higher Self. This is how Spirit works with us.

Most of your Spiritual Guides will change over the course of your lifetime, as you need assistance and understanding on different parts of your journey. However, the one energy that never changes is your Guardian Angel. This energy is dedicated to looking after you and only you from the day you are born until the day that you pass over to the Spiritual Realms. This particular Guide is a highly evolved being that knows exactly how to look after you, and everything there is to know about you. Your Guardian Angel knows you better than you know yourself. It is their job to report back to the Higher Energies and to the other Spiritual Helpers around you, as to how to best help and support you along your soul's journey. The other Guides around you will come and go. For instance, when you decide what you wish to study at school, you will have a Guide who is an expert on that subject come and work with you. Not only are you receiving education and guidance from the conscious world in the form of teachers and peers, you are also being taught, on a soul and subconscious level, other things that you need to know to master the choices you have made.

There is one very firm and concrete rule between the Earth plane and the Spiritual Realms and that is that those who guide and support us from the other side of the veil are NOT allowed to interfere with our free will. Therefore, if we need help, we must learn to ask for it. Complaining about your life, and/or despairing over your life, is not asking. Be aware of this when you need guidance – you must ask for it. To ask is simple. There is no special mantra or certain words you must use. All you must do is ask respectfully, either within your own head or out loud, for what you need, and to give thanks for this. And you always need to add NOW. The Spirit world and our world have a very different outlook on what "time" is.

There are two very important things to remember when asking for help. Firstly, even though you are asking for something in your life to happen NOW, it may not be the right time for you. Spirit has the big picture. They know your entire life plan in intricate detail and so they know exactly when you need to get what you need to progress along your soul's journey. This may sound unfair and illogical, but when you really think about it, if you knew everything you chose to go through, experience and be in a lifetime, chances are you would run a mile from most of that learning or sabotage it in some way, due to the fears you experience here. Using the scenario of the young man who ended up choosing to take his life (mentioned in Chapter 5 earlier in this book), you can see that if he was fully aware of what he had chosen to go through to learn and evolve in this lifetime, there is no way he would have allowed it to happen. When we block our learning or run away from it, we not only stop our ascension in this lifetime, we may also have to come back to repeat these same lessons all over again.

The planets move in Direct and Retrograde motions. When they are in Direct motion, we are learning and exploring what is going on around us and outside of us. When a planet is in Retrograde motion, we are learning from our inner selves and from what we have felt and experienced in the past. The most well known Retrograde is Mercury Retrograde - when the planet Mercury moves from Direct to Retrograde motion. Mercury turns Retrograde around 3 times every year for approximately 3 weeks each time. Mercury being the planet of communication and thinking keeps us busy when he is Direct by presenting us with information, opinions and action and if we were to always be in this energy, we would exhaust ourselves and fail to understand the true meaning of all that is going on in our lives. During Mercury Retrograde, we are being asked to slow down, re-visit our communications and our actions, and to re-think and re-assess our direction in life and how we are to get there; it's basically our due diligence time. Mercury Retrograde tends to be better known for being disruptive, mischievous and just downright annoying. Because we all live such busy lives in an ever-busy world, the Mercury Retrograde is seen by us as a spanner in the works where nothing goes to plan. However, this is not the intention. We are being given a much needed and invaluable opportunity to slow down, re-group and NOT DO for a while. The more we can embrace this Retrograde, and all other Retrograde periods, and just go with the flow the better use we make of them, and the more confident and prepared we will be to move forward and take action once they are over. And a word of advice: because we are being asked to slow down and take a closer look at things, it is NEVER a good idea to sign any contracts, make any permanent decisions, invest in anything expensive (especially electrical equipment), or do too much travel during a Mercury Retrograde. Chances are all such things will need to be re-negotiated, re-assessed, and that expensive item that you SO thought you needed may well be not as necessary as you thought once this period is over. And when it comes to travel, you can expect delays and breakdowns as well.

When a planet is in Retrograde when we are born, it is visible as such in our Natal Charts and has a slightly different meaning. Retrograde lessons in our Natal Charts are what we call "past life lessons". They are things that we chose to do in one lifetime and did not succeed at due to fears and self-imposed limitations, and so we often choose to come back to the earth plane to learn these lessons again. The challenge for you here is that when you decide to learn something again, due to not learning it the first time, you choose to make it 100 times harder than it was before. If we once again use that scenario of the young man who ended up taking his life (Chapter 5), it would have been in his previous journeys to the earth plane that he tried to master self-worth and self-confidence, probably by simply having to stick up for himself in certain classroom situations, or by having the life-changing experience of making a profound difference in someone else's life. But in those lifetimes, he allowed fear to have control over him, rather than believing in himself and his Higher Self connection. This is why, in the scenario I gave to you earlier, the experiences he chose were so hard and harsh by our standards. When he was in Spirit making those choices, he really believed that once he was in his physical body existing here, he would see the light and conquer the fears and lessons.

In your life plan or Natal Chart, it can be seen very clearly what past life lessons you have chosen to look at and learn again in this lifetime. Your 12th House, for instance, carries the energy of the Past – past the lifetime you are currently living, and the past life energy you are bringing through with you from other lifetimes. Your Nodes also represent your past lives, and these actually show you your most recent relevant past life to the one you are currently living. We do not reincarnate chronologically. We reincarnate in past eras and times as well as in future ones, as it's not about "time", it's about what is available in a certain era, place, and society that can help your soul to learn and evolve. The other clues that are present in your Natal Chart that can help you to understand and master past life lessons are the Retrogrades. If you are born at a time when a planet is in retrograde motion, then you will be choosing to be born with past life lessons to do with where that planet is sitting in your Natal Chart – as in which House and which sign of the zodiac it is sitting in. The planet denotes the lesson, the House where the lesson will present itself to you to be learned, and the sign of the zodiac tells you how you will go about learning this lesson. This is true of all placements in your Chart, whether they are Retrograde or not.

Past Life lessons and the energy they contain are not just about what you have failed to learn that was hard and uncomfortable for you. Past Life lessons also show where you have had strengths before, and where you have hidden talents and gifts that you have used before, that are still at your disposal in this lifetime. As souls evolving through many lifetimes and many experiences, we have acquired and developed gifts and talents along the way. In most lifetimes we will get a chance to use these, but sometimes we do not realise the gifts we possess; they become repressed by the external conditions around us, or by the way we feel about ourselves. These gifts and talents do not go away or disappear – they just wait within our soul memories for the opportunity to be reactivated and used by us for our highest good. Just like my experiences with astrology.

We have in the course of our many lifetimes learned things, and these are stored away in our cell and soul memories. It is these memories that you can tap into to achieve your dreams and goals in any lifetime. Those things that we learned and/or experienced before in other lifetimes, tend to be easy for us to master in this lifetime simply because they are not new learning. They are the recovery of old memories that we used successfully in the past and can now use to take care of and advance ourselves in life once again.

There are, of course, always new things we need to learn. It is these new things that can present the most difficulties for us and create the deepest fear. If your soul has never learned or mastered a certain skill in another lifetime, then it is not nearly as good at guiding you and supporting you to do this in this lifetime. In situations like this, your Guides and Helpers have a lot more work to do, to bring to you the spiritual "specialist" in that area, and to help you to keep your confidence up and keep going when you feel like it's a real struggle to do so.

# CHAPTER 16

# THE STAR CHILD

*("Let's not make musicians into mathematicians.")*

This brings me to the next topic within our soul's journeys on the earth plane – our childhood. It is my belief that all children, up until the age of 6 - 8 years old, remember their past lives, their true calling, and who they truly are. As I stated earlier, it is the parents and families we chose who have the most influence and power over us up until around the age of 6 years. Until then we are open vessels, and within that openness we are willing and able to express who we truly are. Therefore, what children do in play or what they gravitate towards in life, of their own choosing, is more often than not their soul's purpose in this lifetime. Just look at what happened to me with my childhood Astrology Project! When left to their own devices and choices, children will always do what they love best and what they know they are good at. They are fully aware of their natural talents, but of course do not always know exactly how to express these in the Society they live in. As I said, when you find them playing or ask them what they would like to play with or do, they will more often than not want to do what "feels" right for them. Children are highly intuitive, so they are not only picking up on what their Spiritual Helpers are teaching them, they are also picking up on the roles of those around them as well. An interesting and fun thing to do with your children or any other children that you have in your life is to get them to tell you a story. Many children have stories read to them at night before they go to sleep as part of their evening ritual, and so this is a good time and space to ask the child to tell you a story instead. Nine times of out ten, the story they tell you will be to do with a past life they experienced and what they are remembering from being in that other time and place. They can, of course, also tell you a story about the day they just had or something they did last week. But when you hear something from their mouths at any given time that you do not understand or cannot place, they are reliving a soul memory. This information can be invaluable to you in understanding your child better.

We all arrive on the earth plane with our own gifts and talents, strengths and weaknesses, and lessons to learn that are ours and ours alone. In an ideal world, after their child is born every parent should be given a copy of the child's Natal Chart and its practical and esoteric interpretation. Just because your child is born into your family, which may have always owned the local seafood restaurant, does not mean that they are born to work there or develop skills in that area. They have their own agenda, their own mission, and their own soul's journey. In reading and understanding their Natal Chart or life purpose, parents and caregivers can see what this soul is choosing to learn, experience and be in this lifetime, and then guide and support them towards their goals, rather than deciding for them what they should or should not be doing with their lives. Give your children the freedom to choose their lives in the physical so as they can manifest what they have planned in the spiritual. This is the greatest gift, along with the unconditional love that you give to your child. Yes, they are helpless and need lots of boundaries, care and support as they grow – but they are also, like you, armed with incredible power and talent that is just waiting to be released or activated so as they can continue their soul's journey and evolve through experiences on the earth plane. Remember we ALL choose our lives before we are born. The more guidance and support we have for the choices we made, the more likely we are to succeed and evolve.

# CHAPTER 17

# THE MIRRORS AROUND YOU

*("I look like that! eewh!")*

Coming back once again to the choices we made before we were born, it is the people we chose to put in our lives who will teach us the most. Everyone in your life is a mirror for you, as you have put them there to teach you by looking at your own reflection. Sometimes in life we come across those whom we really dislike; these are the people who usually teach us our greatest life lessons. Such people display the full-blown effect of something that you also have, or that you contain a small portion of. It is not nice to see reflected back at you what you so deeply dislike, distrust or fear about who you truly are. These people, whom you chose to put in your life and who readily accepted this contact with you as they are also here to learn, are integral to your growth and understanding as a soul on a journey. The more honest and transparent you can be with yourself, the more quickly you will learn and the faster your soul will evolve. It may not be nice to see yourself reflected back in a negative way; but the more you deny this or try to turn away from it, the more of such people you will attract until you are willing to look at what you have to learn here and change that reflection.

*What you resist, persists....*

It is said that you cannot recognise an attitude or emotion in another soul unless you yourself also contain that attitude or emotion. It is the

112

recognition of this, usually at a soul level, that allows us to compute and resonate with this energy – whether we like it or not. The biggest arena where this can play out is the arena of judgement. Humanity is so quick to judge anything or anyone that it does not understand or that causes it fear. More often than not, those who judge others the most harshly are those who judge themselves the most harshly too.

As challenging as these reflections can be, the beautiful thing is that we also reflect back and forth to one another the more beautiful, loving, peaceful and positive aspects of ourselves too. When you recognise beauty, compassion, understanding and love in another soul, you can know that you too have such aspects within yourself and what better qualities to expand upon than these.

From an astrological perspective, you will keep attracting the same sign of the zodiac to you until you learn what they have to teach you. We can all identify with times in our lives when we look around to see whom we are surrounded by and find that they are all mostly of the same sign of the zodiac. These people can be anything from family members (lifelong lessons), to friends, neighbours, colleagues or team members. For instance, you might be a Capricorn, a sign of the zodiac renowned for its logic, detachment and sometimes-blind ambition, and you keep finding yourself meeting people who are mainly Cancerians. It is good to look at what attributes the Cancerians have that you, as a Capricorn, are lacking in, such as compassion, understanding and empathy. Or if you are a Scorpio (over-sensitive, controlling and power hungry), you could suddenly find yourself surrounded by the easy-going energy of Aquarians who help you to understand how to detach from emotions, not sweat the small stuff and go with the flow more.

If you can take a step back and out of yourself and look at those around you in this way, you can be assured that you are taking advantage of every opportunity the Universe is bringing your way, to better yourself and to learn your life lessons.

# CHAPTER 18

# THE POWER OF DETACHMENT

*("Thanks, but I'm getting off this crazy roller-coaster ride.")*

The ultimate tool we are encouraged to use in life is the ability to detach from what is going on emotionally and look at it objectively. When we do this, we see the lesson as being the most important thing and not the emotion it is making us feel. To do this, start by observing yourself. Rather than thinking "that really hurt my feelings and now I feel sad" think "that really hurt (your name's) feelings". "Why has that affected her so much and why does she feel sad now?" Then you start stripping it down. Most of what we feel usually comes down to one or two deep hurts or wounds within ourselves that we have come here to heal.

So, back to the scenario of you feeling hurt... let's say you are hurt because someone criticised your work. If we strip that back it becomes – you are hurt because someone made you feel like you weren't good enough. The next question you can ask yourself is, "What else in your life has made you feel that way?" and then, "When else have these feelings come up in your life and what triggered them?" Now that you know that not feeling good enough is an issue for you, how can you go about healing it? You allow yourself to go deeper and to find the root of the problem so you can heal the initial wound and not just the resulting symptoms.

This is also where astrology comes in. The more you understand your astrological make-up, the more you can see why you feel/react this way, and what you can do to change that energy around. If you are born sensitive it is who you are and you see being sensitive as hard work, as you tend to feel things much more deeply than others do, BUT, being sensitive also allows you to be intuitive and understanding of others and very creative too. It's all about directing those negatives into positives and using the energy for your highest good rather than for your suffering.

You are here by choice, not by chance and there is a map for all that you wish to explore and experience. You don't have to feel like you are going around in circles or even going nowhere. Once you have that awareness and understanding, your life will change and it can and will evolve into the life you wish it to be, the life you originally planned it to be. But you have to step it up and you have to take RESPONSIBILITY.

Spiritual teachers around the world all agree that astrology is the key to understanding your life and all that you have chosen. Without this, it is like hiking without a map, sailing without a compass or flying without wings. Until you understand who you truly are and what you are here for, you bump and scrape through life from pillar to post. You live constantly in fear of what might happen next and what others think. You try to be like and emulate those that you admire and/or are jealous of. You see yourself as being the victim and you are well and truly stuck on that crazy emotional roller coaster holding on for dear life and with no idea how to get off.

Through taking the brave and powerful step to explore who you truly are and what makes you tick, you take the biggest step forward you can ever take along your spiritual journey. I can assure you that the rewards that come for being brave enough to do so are more than a million times worth every bit of struggle and every bit of hard effort you put into being who you truly are.

*"The spiritual path is the hardest path you will ever walk, and only 1 out of every 1,000 souls who have chosen to come here to walk this path, ever make it." Master Maitreya*

This path is not hard because of what may happen around you. It's hard because you must look at, deal with, accept, forgive and love the real you – warts, wrinkly bits, ugly bits and all. You must go deep within yourself to identify why you feel the way you do, why you react the way you do, and where it all has come from. And you must be aware of and acknowledge the power of past life energy and how much it affects all that you do and feel in this lifetime. You must learn to differentiate between what was then and what is now.

# CHAPTER 19

# FINDING THE REAL YOU

*("Hello beautiful! Welcome to your life.")*

Inside of you is the answer to every question you have ever had about your life. When the time is right, this information will resonate with you, and become the most powerful tool you have to master self-love and self-worth so as you can BE the beautiful soul you truly are, and not what Society and your own insecurities make you feel you should be.

*"All you will ever find deep inside of yourself are the fears you have buried and the gifts you have yet to acknowledge"*

You are not here to be that famous film star on the silver screen, and you are not here to be that brilliant scientist on the TV. Those roles are already taken, and recreating yourself in their images is not honouring or doing justice to the true you and what you have to offer that is yours, and yours alone. There is only one you, no one else has been made in the same way, and you are perfect just as you are.

We are all born with own talents and skills and sometimes these are not what you would like them to be or what others around you think they should be. But they are real, and they are yours and most importantly YOU CHOSE THEM! Doesn't it make sense to go deep, to get to know yourself so you can find those real and natural skills you lovingly and thoughtfully brought with you into this lifetime, so you can share these with the world?

You are never alone in this world either. Although it may feel very much like that at times, you are always surrounded by your Spiritual Guides and Helpers supporting you, guiding you and loving you every step of the way. Along with this highly qualified and devoted help, you have your Blue Print – your Natal Chart – the plan and insight for this life you have chosen.

We co-create with the Universe. This means that we always have support, assistance and guidance along our soul journey; we just need to learn to ask and then get out of our own way. Like attracts like. Your life is yours to not only enjoy but to be the best you can possibly be, and your happiness, peace and success are your responsibility, and your responsibility alone.

You are a God-spark of infinite possibilities and you are loved, honoured and respected more than you will ever know by all in the Spiritual Realms. This is your life, your journey and your voyage of discovery and you chose every aspect of it. So, wake up and embrace it ALL, because it really is "ALL YOUR FAULT".

© Deidre Wilton

# ACKNOWLEDGEMENTS

There are some amazing people in my life – both on the earth plane and in Spirit that I would like to thank from the bottom of my heart for their input into this book and into my life.

Firstly, to my daughters for putting up with their weird mother. Although you know you chose me, I am sure there are times when you really wonder…? I love you both and am so grateful that you chose me to be your mother.

Secondly, I would like to thank my soulmate Marg Fitches for being my rock, my unconditional support and the other sock to our very odd pair. You left the earth plane over 3 years ago now and I still feel your immense loving energy and know how very proud of me you must be for getting this Book out there.

I would also like to thank Margaret McElroy who passed into the Spiritual Realms nearly 2 years ago, and the Master Maitreya for all your love, support and wisdom. This book is written as much by Spirit as it is by me, and I am incredibly grateful for all that you both channel through me into words and energy that I can share with the world.

For the photographs on the front and back covers of this Book I have the marvellous and inspirational Christine Spring to thank. Your photographic talents are amazing, and one can only look and feel beautiful when you are behind the lens.

The beautiful front and back cover designs are the work of the very talented Yoran Nap. This young man has so far to go in this world and I am extremely thankful to him for all his patience with me changing my mind every 5 minutes, and for all the dedication and devotion he puts into his design work.

And finally I would like to thank Linda Zeppa – "Editor Extraordinaire" for all her hard work. Thank you for creating an amazing Book out of my manuscript and making sense out of the messages I have tried so hard to get across. It's really thanks to you Linda that this Book makes any sense at all!!

# ABOUT THE AUTHOR

Deidre Wilton is a renowned Esoteric Astrologer, Metaphysical Teacher and Spiritual Counsellor, who has been guiding and assisting people from all over the world for more than 15 years. She studied with world renowned medium and deep trance channel for the Ascended Master, Maitreya – Margaret McElroy (Birkin) for many years, and has gained a vast array of knowledge and experience which she generously shares with her students and clients around the world.

Deidre teaches Workshops, run Courses, and meets and works privately with thousands of clients around the world on her journey to bring the wisdom and understanding of astrology and metaphysics to the earth plane. Deidre believes passionately that we are all here for a reason and that the more we can understand and accept who we truly are, the more equipped we will be to create and embrace happy, fulfilled and empowered lives on every level. Through her own personal journey and all that she has been taught, Deidre has created her own unique way of teaching and interpreting astrology that changes the lives and awareness of everyone she works with.

An amazingly accurate Intuitive as well as Astrologer, Deidre is as well-known for her individual Readings and forecasts, as she is for her Workshops and teachings.

Deidre created Star-Wise Clairvoyant Astrology in 2003 (www. star-wise.com) as a platform from which she could reach out and share with souls all around the world her knowledge, wisdom and understanding of the world of Spirit and Astrology. And with the release of her first book "It's All Your Fault" she hopes to touch and change countless more lives and set thousands of souls on their path to embracing their lives and finding power and joy in all that they do.

Printed in the United States
By Bookmasters